SATANIC COLONIZATION
AND SPIRITUAL
EMANCIPATION

Moses O. Oluwole, PhD

SATANIC COLONIZATION
AND **SPIRITUAL**
EMANCIPATION

Moses O. Oluwole, PhD

Kravitz & Sons
INNOVATORS IN PUBLISHING, MARKETING AND ADVERTISING

Kravitz and Sons LLC
204 E Arlington Blvd. Suite B
Greenville, NC 27858

Published by Kravitz and Sons LLC.

Spirituality and Psychology

ISBN: 979-8-89639-614-7 (sc)
ISBN: 979-8-89639-613-0 (e)

Library of Congress Control Number: 2026901389

THIS BOOK IS DEDICATED FIRST AND FOREMOST
TO MY LORD AND SAVIOR JESUS CHRIST

AND

SECONDLY TO MY LOVING DARLING,
DOYIN,

FOR THE LOVING CARE, UNDERSTANDING, PATIENCE,
HOME AND FELLOWSHIP IN THE MINISTRY

TO WHICH THE LORD HAS CALLED US.

ACKNOWLEDGMENT

I have to start by thanking my Supreme Teacher, Helper and Friend, God the Holy Spirit, for giving me the topic and all needed inspiration to carry out this noble project.

Secondly, thanks to my awesome darling, Doyin, who has been very supportive right from reading the early drafts to giving me wise counsel at every stage of the project up to the cover design. She was as important to this book getting done as I was. Thank you so much my beautiful darling.

TABLE OF CONTENTS

ABOUT THE AUTHOR

Moses Oluwole, PhD, is a scientist, with specialization in industrial chemistry. For several decades, he has dedicated himself to international Christian education through Model Prayer Ministries International, which he and his wife co-founded in 2000 with Bishop Henry Ndozi-Okia while they were resident in Namibia, Southern Africa. Model Prayer Ministries International has branches in India, Pakistan, the United States and various African countries. Moses has authored several Christian books to spread the glorious Gospel of our Lord Jesus Christ to people around the world. This book is just another of those attempts. It is his heart's desire and prayer that after reading this book, people will get to know the only true God, the Creator of heaven and earth, the One Who rules in the affairs of men.

He is married to his beautiful and intelligent wife, Doyin. They are blessed with four very successful children and four adorable grandchildren.

PREFACE

"*The Spirit of the Lord is upon me, because he hath anointed me to preach the gospel to the poor; he hath sent me to heal the brokenhearted, to preach deliverance to the captives, and recovering of sight to the blind, to set at liberty them that are bruised, to preach the acceptable year of the Lord*" **(Lk. 4:18-19).**

Satan, the archenemy of man, is crafty and relentless in his attacks against humanity. Satanic oppression is real, and wickedness is universal, but the victory of our Lord Jesus Christ is more evident in every sphere of life. Satan consistently exerts his power, influence, and strategy on man in order to establish his evil kingdom in the hearts of humans. He is slow and systematic; hence, he is gaining grounds as he keeps captivating innocent people and accomplishing his evil schemes on earth.

Unknown to people, Satan sits like a king, enthroned in their inward parts, thereby controlling them to do things that are contrary to God's will and detestable to Him and humanity.

"And even as they did not like to retain God in their knowledge, God gave them over to a reprobate mind, to do those things which are not convenient" **(Rom. 1:28).**

It is quite disheartening to see people who were originally created in the image of God straying out of His will and ordinances; committing atrocities; walking in total disobedience to God's commandments; and deliberately treading the path of destruction.

Undoubtedly, people caught by the web of Satan are generally known to be careless, callous, corrupt and contaminated with odious sins ranging from killing to idolatry. Pathetically, Satan is subtly introducing his schemes and sins to the world on a daily basis. More pitiable is the fact that most people have not discerned the operations of Satan; hence, they have become victims of their ignorance.

Today, Satan has subtly infiltrated every aspect of human life to the extent that it almost seems inescapable, at least from what can be perceived from the state of our world. Evidently, the rebellious strategy of Satan to establish his government on earth has been from the beginning. In the Garden of Eden, God gave man the mandate to be fruitful and multiply, not just in terms of number but also to herald His love and grace to the whole world. However, Satan has badly tainted the world, and he is vehemently fighting this divine purpose in today's generation.

Sadly, people no longer call sin what it is. For example, when they lie, they simply say they "misspoke." Also, when they commit abortion, they call it "pro-choice." They deliberately trivialize the gravity of sin. However, the Bible clearly reveals to us the painful and inevitable consequences of sin. They ignore the grave dangers of their sins and the accompanying destructive consequences. The Bible says, *"The soul that sinneth shall die."*

Unsurprisingly, the world is now experiencing a growing number of deadly diseases with no known cure. The incidence at the Garden of Eden does not only show the disobedience of man and the mercy of God but also unveiled the beginning of satanic colonization. Sin is the perversion of humankind that widens the gap between man and God, and that became evident when Adam and Eve sinned and were banished from the glorious garden.

It is imperative to notice the amazing love of God; despite sending them out of the garden, He continually watched over them and provided for them and their descendants. He devised a complete plan through which He would save humankind and remove the barrier once again.

Graciously, God intervened and redeemed man by sending His one and only begotten Son, Jesus Christ, to deliver and save mankind from sin. But this was not an afterthought; rather it was predetermined. Before the fall of man, God had a backup plan for man's deliverance, salvation, and restoration in the form of a sinless Lamb: Jesus Christ who was slain before the foundation of the world. As soon as sin manifested, God implemented His backup plan.

"And she shall bring forth a son, and thou shalt call his name Jesus: for he shall save his people from their sins" (**Mt. 1:21**).

This book gives an amazing revelation of how God initiated, executed and brought His redemption plan to completion.

"For thou wast slain, and hast redeemed us to God by thy blood out of every kindred, and tongue, and people, and nation" **(Rev. 5:9).**

The Scripture expressly states that Satan's plan to distort God's image in man still continues, as long as there are unbelieving souls and wandering hearts on earth. Satan can still manage to establish his kingdom through evil people. However, Jesus, the wonderful son of God, came in human form and trampled the devil under His feet.

"And having spoiled principalities and powers, he made a show of them openly, triumphing over them in it" **(Col. 2:15).**

Therefore, through the pages of this golden book, you will encounter deep insight and uncommon revelation about what the Bible teaches on satanic colonization and how to gain unlimited freedom from his grip. This book contains a laconic story about the creation of man, his affection, exaltation, his fall and separation from God's presence. You will also find how God's promise of ultimate victory over sin and Satan gives hope to the fallen humanity, as well as records of men and women of faith who walked triumphantly on earth.

Satan's plan of entrapment began in Eden, but it has been frequently implemented from one generation to another. He is hell-bent on establishing his government in the hearts of humans.

Symbolically, the Lamb was planted as seed in various chosen vessels, starting from Abel, Seth, Enoch, Noah, Abraham, Isaac, Jacob, and several others, till the miraculous conception and birth of our Savior, Jesus Christ, through a virgin in the lineage of David.

Nevertheless, Satan still succeeded in getting many people captivated throughout the world, even after the depravity of Noah's time, which had resulted in total destruction of the world by God's wrath. Despite this, man continued to wallow in sin due to satanic influence, manipulation, and control.

Pathetically, the Bible shows us how God left the depraved generation, after prolonged patience and mercy. God ignored them in their sins so that they could freely carry out all their evil desires. Ignorantly, people engaged themselves in idolatry, bowing down to graven images which they crafted through their vile imaginations. They threw caution to the air and defiantly committed murder, abortion, and homosexuality, which totally distort the glorious image that God has bestowed on man. (See Romans 1:18-32).

In our contemporary world, sin has become a celebrated treasure and the fear of God is fading and melting away like ice at noonday.

Graciously, the good news is that when our Lord Jesus paid the supreme price of our redemption at Calvary, He seized all power from Satan. He restored it to us and subsequently sealed our victory by sending the Holy Spirit to establish the Kingdom of God in the hearts of those who surrender their lives to Jesus Christ.

"Behold, I give unto you power to tread on serpents and scorpions, and over all the power of the enemy; and nothing shall by any means hurt you" **(Lk. 10:19).**

Emphatically, He has given authority to believers over Satan and has safeguarded the hearts that call out to Him by faith.

The aim of writing this book is to sensitize believers and equip the saints of God about the devices of Satan and to flood their hearts with the knowledge of our victory in Christ Jesus. This will inevitably empower believers to fight the good fight of faith and enjoy freedom from satanic colonization. Apostle Paul clearly revealed in 2 Corinthians 2:11 that, *"Lest Satan should get an advantage of us: for we are not ignorant of his devices."*

It is imperative that you know the devices of Satan, as well as your worth in Christ Jesus, and the need to keep your gaze fixated on Him. This awareness will culminate in your defense against the pranks of the enemies as well as help you stand your ground firmly by faith in Christ Jesus.

"And ye shall know the truth, and the truth shall make you free" (**Jn. 8:32**).

It is my earnest prayer that this book will be a source of blessing to you, just as it has been a blessing to me in the process of writing and compilation.

CHAPTER 1

ACQUIRING THE MIND OF CHRIST

*S*o, God created man in his own image, in the image of God created he him; male and female created he them" (**Gen. 1:27**).

At creation, God intentionally made man in His own image to enable man display His divine qualities and attributes. Nothing gives us greater joy than imagining the perfection of God embodied in our mortal bodies. Amazingly, at creation, we were a complete replica of God in every manner: in purity, love, and immortality. Undoubtedly, this was the perfect expression of the divine plan of God. There is no better way to describe or demonstrate His love for mankind at the beginning of the age other than bringing us into His unspeakable glory and marvelous image. Ultimately, He distinguished man from other creatures by crowning us with His glory, honor, likeness, and image.

"What is man, that thou art mindful of him? And the son of man, that thou visitest him? For thou hast made him a little lower than the angels, and hast crowned him with glory and honor. Thou madest him to have dominion over the works of thy hands; thou hast put all things under his feet" (**Ps. 8:4-6**).

Furthermore, He gave unlimited authority and dominion to man. In other words, He made man the ruler of the entire world. Graciously, He also instructed man to be fruitful and multiply.

"And God blessed them, and God said unto them, be fruitful, and multiply, and replenish the earth, and subdue it: and have dominion over the fish of the sea, and over the fowl of the air, and over every living thing that moveth upon the earth" **(Gen. 1:28).** However, Satan's attempt to mar the image of God and to usurp His authority has been his number one agenda since the beginning of creation.

In the story of Adam and Eve, when God strictly forbade them from eating the fruit of the tree of knowledge because it would surely lead to their death, Satan showed up and successfully deceived them into disobedience against God (see Genesis 3:1-24). Alas, Satan used guile to lure man into disobedience. He spurred curiosity in the heart of Eve and ultimately led her astray. Deceptively, Satan said, "You will not surely die."

Despite the blessing of having all the fruits of the garden, coupled with unhindered access to the refreshing presence of God, man made a poor choice and naively decided to give in to Satan's deceptive strategy. Regrettably, they ate the forbidden fruit and consequently invited death into their lives. Again, they were not only banished from the glorious garden: they equally lost the glorious image that God endued them with.

Truly, God is righteous, and no sinful being can dwell in His presence. Thus, this was the tale of how man lost God's image and subsequently became corrupted by sin. Thereafter, man drifted so badly, thereby, inculcating several attributes of Satan and shedding off the glorious image of God.

"Ye are of your father the devil, and the lusts of your father ye will do: he was a murderer from the beginning, and abode not in the truth, because there is no truth in him. When he speaketh a lie, he speaketh of his own: for he is a liar, and the father of it" **(Jn. 8:44).**

THE SPREAD OF SIN

Following the events that took place in the Garden of Eden, sin became deeply rooted and virulently spread across the whole world. Satan craftily took over the authority that God had given to man, who was created to be His earthly representative. Subsequently, hatred, lust, greed and several other sins began to reign.

Moreover, there are several examples of people and leaders chosen and appointed by God in the Holy Bible. Unfortunately, some of them fell as prey to the wiles of Satan, and their power, virtues, fame, and relevance dwindled and drastically crashed.

Obviously, as the world is aging, man's depravity is growing. This anomaly further widened the gap between man and God. By and large, human beings had to perform animal sacrifices in order to appease God and seek for forgiveness of sin. Despite this, God stayed afar from them. They could only access Him in the Holy of Holies where He manifested His presence to them.

After a prolonged time of trial and error, characterized by pains, sicknesses, calamities, and death, there came a Savior in divine and human form (complete man and perfect

God), who showed mankind that there is hope for the sinking, stinking and erring world. He emphatically proved that there was hope and ultimately regained the lost image. He displayed that perfect image through His words, actions, teachings, and works. He is the Son of God, Jesus Christ our Lord and Savior, who came to restore mankind to God.

"Then answered Jesus and said unto them, 'Verily, verily, I say unto you, the Son can do nothing of himself, but what he seeth the Father do: for what things soever he doeth, these also doeth the Son likewise. For the Father loveth the Son, and showeth him all things that himself doeth: and he will show him greater works than these, that ye may marvel'" **(Jn. 5:19-20).**

During His earthly ministry, Jesus was the express image of God. Evidently, He only did what He had seen the Father do. He was kind, gentle and merciful towards people and above all, He loved us all even before we accepted His love. He displayed the unconditional love of God which was once present in our hearts. While on earth, He fully exemplified and exhibited that God is love. Despite being a man, He lived a life of love, and now we have seen the possibility of replicating Jesus' kind of love. Once again, God proved that it was possible to be purged of our sins through the atoning blood of Jesus.

HOW TO ACQUIRE THE MIND OF CHRIST

Is it not important for us to be fully armed with the understanding of how to regain the lost image? Having answered this question, then, we can also ask about how we can possess the mind of Christ, so that we can be like Him? Apostle Paul plainly commanded the Philippians,

"Let this mind be in you which was also in Christ Jesus" (**Phil. 2:5**).

Besides, he reiterated that all believers, irrespective of their status and countries of origin, can have the same mind with Jesus.

"For who hath known the mind of the Lord, that he may instruct Him? But we have the mind of Christ" (**1 Cor. 2:16**).

How can we achieve this great and supernatural feat? The answer isn't farfetched; we are delivered and granted freedom by the powerful and precious blood of Jesus. After the death of Jesus, His sinless blood was shed to atone for our sins. The ancient barrier was removed and the veil inhibiting our access to God was rent in two from top to bottom. Therefore, believing Jesus and the efficacy of His blood gives us the full access into God's kingdom.

"In whom ye also trusted, after that ye heard the word of truth, the gospel of your salvation: in whom also, after that ye believed, ye were sealed with that Holy Spirit of promise, which is the earnest of our inheritance until the redemption of the purchased possession, unto the praise of his glory" (**Eph. 1:13-14**).

Affirmatively, our faith in Him qualifies us as partakers of His divine nature, blessings and as well seals us with His Spirit. We are granted access to enjoy His holy presence, which is now closer to us than ever before. His Spirit makes a home in our bodies; hence we become a divine carrier and His power chamber. It is He who forms the image of Christ in us.

"What! know ye not that your body is the temple of the Holy Ghost which is in you, which ye have of God, and ye are not your own?" (**1 Cor. 6:19**).

"I beseech you therefore, brethren, by the mercies of God, that ye present your bodies a living sacrifice, holy, acceptable unto God, which is your reasonable service. And be not conformed to this world: but be ye transformed by the renewing of your mind, that ye may prove what is that good, and acceptable, and perfect, will of God" (**Romans 12:1-2**).

Miraculously, our bodies are living sanctuaries and an extension of His holy tabernacle, where God now dwells as a result of our faith in Jesus Christ.

<u>OUR ACCESS TO REVELATIONS</u>

"For what man knoweth the things of a man, save the spirit of man which is in him? Even so the things of God knoweth no man, but the Spirit of God" (**1 Cor. 2:11**).

The Bible clearly states that the Spirit has the greatest tendency to search, receive and align with the will of God. Therefore, when Apostle Paul said, "we have the mind of Christ," he implied that the Spirit of God that dwells in us, enables us to understand spiritual things that are unknown to ordinary men. Moreover, the Bible indicates that our inner Spirit has unrestricted access to hidden and mysterious secrets. Also, He has the ability to unfold things to us.

"But God hath revealed them unto us by his Spirit: for the Spirit searcheth all things, yea, the deep things of God" (**1 Cor. 2:10**).

As sons and daughters of God, we have been given the grace to know Him, even as a son knows his father, and consequently has full access to the inheritance of his father. Similarly, we have been empowered to know God and as well granted access to His limitless blessings. Now, we can boldly approach His throne, by wearing the image of Christ and stripping off our old man. There is a major exchange of the new life and it is a complete transference of God's grace and righteousness to us.

"For he hath made him to be sin for us, who knew no sin; that we might be made the righteousness of God in him" (**2 Cor. 5:21**).

Therefore, entering into this new life that God intended for us offers us an inexplicable opportunity to be like Him on a daily basis, not just in word, but in action and lifestyle.

"Therefore if any man be in Christ, he is a new creature: old things are passed away; behold, all things are become new" (**2 Cor. 5:17**).

END TIME STRUGGLE

As the world moves close to its inevitable end and as the day of the Lord approaches, Satan is digging deeper into the hearts of men to lead them astray and lure them to the path that leads to utter destruction.

Jesus speaks in John 10:10 that, *"The thief cometh not, but for to steal, and to kill, and to destroy: I am come that they might have life, and that they might have it more abundantly."*

This verse of the Holy Bible artistically paints the portrait of Satan's mission, pinpointing his destructive agenda. The primary mission of Satan has never and can never change. He came to steal the image of God, causing death to dominate man and as well destroy his bond and relationship with the Father. Unknown to us, he placed a veil on our eyes, thereby blinding us to God's grace and luring us into sin, like Adam and Eve. Being a rebel and lover of power, Satan greatly desired the place of God, and that was the ambition he planted into the heart of the first man and woman.

"And when the woman saw that the tree was good for food, and that it was pleasant to the eyes, and a tree to be desired to make one wise, she took of the fruit thereof, and did eat..." **(Gen. 3:6).**

From the Scripture above, there are three conspicuous characteristics of the forbidden fruit, which succinctly describe the nature of sin. The fruit was good for food, pleasant to the eyes and was desirable to make one wise. Without any doubt, sin works in similar ways to these fundamental characteristics. We are drawn to it by its apparent beauty and the temporal benefits it presents to us. Moreover, the third characteristic is that it makes one wise. However, it is a lie that sin makes us wise. Sin was deceptively presented to Adam and Eve in an attractive manner that they naively wanted to acquire such wisdom. The deceiver calmly and deceptively whispered lies to them, giving a false assurance.

"And the serpent said unto the woman, ye shall not surely die: for God doth know that in the day ye eat thereof, then your eyes shall be opened, and ye shall be as gods, knowing good and evil" **(Gen. 3:4-5).**

At this point, humans have been baited by Satan and were at the verge of taking on the image of Satan. More worrisome is the fact that they desired to be "like God." Unknown to them that they were originally like God, but Satan's lie abruptly robbed them of the likeness they shared with God.

Similar to Eden's experience, the Tree of Knowledge and the Tree of Life represent two kingdoms in our lives. The first one leads to death, and it is the kingdom that Satan had earlier established in the world. Contrarily, the second one is the Kingdom of God that offers abundant and everlasting life.

As always, the choice is ours and we need to choose wisely, so that we may be able to acquire the image of Christ and radiate His glory.

FOLLOW THE PRINCIPLES OF CHRIST

An intelligent man once opined that the easiest subject to pass is mathematics. He stressed that all you have to do to excel in mathematics is to follow examples given by the teacher. Similarly, all we need to do if we must excel in our walk with Jesus Christ is to follow His steps and principles.

Christ became our perfect example, the author and finisher of our faith. Therefore, we need to take after Him.

"Therefore, as by the offense of one judgment came upon all men to condemnation; even so by the righteousness of one the free gift came upon all men unto justification of life. For as by one man's disobedience many were made sinners, so by the obedience of one shall many be made righteous" **(Rom. 5:18-19).**

Adam lost the image of God through disobedience, thereby making subsequent generations become heirs and victims of sin. Conversely, the image of God in Christ makes every believer a new creation through His Spirit.

THE REGENERATED LIFE

Thus, to possess the mind of Christ, the individual must be born again. Being born again or regenerated implies believing in the Lord Jesus Christ and forsaking the old and satanic path of doom, to follow God's ways for the rest of one's life. Be reminded, after the genuine repentance of the prodigal son, he never returned to his sin, rather he lived as an obedient son.

Our regeneration invites and makes the Holy Spirit to come and dwell in us so that we may know what the perfect will of God is, and as well seek to do what Jesus did. After experiencing the new birth, we begin to produce the fruits of the Spirit namely: love, joy, peace, patience, kindness, goodness, faithfulness, gentleness, and self-control, which make us an express image of Christ.

Now, while we are seeking to imitate Him, it is out of sheer obedience and love that comes on us through the Holy Spirit that confers His image and possibilities on us. In this transformed state, we will always seek the glory of God and never attempt to share that glory with Him.

For example, when a baby is in the womb, it's attached to his mother by the placenta and umbilical cord. The purpose of the umbilical cord is to transfer food, oxygen, and nutrients necessary for the nourishment, growth, and development of the fetus from the mother. Similarly, the Spirit of God acts as an umbilical cord by becoming a medium for transferring His life-giving power to believers. Furthermore, the close connection between us and God keeps us focused to fulfill God's will in everything we do.

LEARN TO ABIDE

"Abide in me, and I in you. As the branch cannot bear fruit of itself, except it abide in the vine; no more can ye, except ye abide in me" (**Jn. 15:4**).

Striving to bear fruit and struggling to do good without connecting to Jesus Christ is an impossible task because all goodness stems from Him. He is the vine from which we derive our sustenance so that we can spread like branches and bear acceptable fruits of the Spirit.

God desires fruitfulness; His love for fruitfulness became the premise upon which He released His blessing upon Adam and Eve.

"Be fruitful and multiply, and subdue the earth."

As Christians, we are also commanded to be fruitful, multiply and subdue the earth by expressing the image of Jesus Christ; that is, by loving and serving others as we fulfill the Great Commission. The Holy Spirit helps us greatly and plants the desire for obedience in us. This obedience is from the depths of our hearts and becomes visible in our actions. What we feed into our minds and think about greatly influences our behavior. This, in turn, determines the impact we have on other people's lives. All our actions originate from our hearts. *"A good man out of the good treasure of his heart bringeth forth that which is good; and an evil man out of the evil treasure of his heart bringeth forth that which is evil: for of the abundance of the heart his mouth speaketh"* **(Lk. 6:45).**

Therefore, in order to be like Christ, we need to think like Him at all times. Mandatorily, we must seek to understand why it is necessary for us to be Christ-like. This truth will help our walk with God and emblazon us with the conviction that doesn't falter but stands strong during trials.

BENEFITS OF HAVING THE MIND OF CHRIST

1. To know God

When the Spirit of God resides in our hearts, He reveals the deep and hidden mysteries of God to us. He unveils and interprets God's word and enlightens us about the truth of His Majesty.

"That their hearts might be comforted, being knit together in love, and unto all riches of the full assurance of understanding, to the acknowledgment of the mystery of God, and of the Father, and of Christ, in whom are hid all the treasures of wisdom and knowledge" **(Col. 2:2-3).**

We get to know God more deeply and intimately, therefore, we can effortlessly display His nature in our actions.

2. Growing fellowship with God

Possessing the mind of Christ will not only help us to know Him better, but it also increases our intimacy with Him. This will bring us to the point that we understand God's will for our lives. More importantly, seeking His will becomes our utmost priority and we reason in accordance with His word and make it the compass of our actions.

"O God, thou art my God; early will I seek thee: my soul thirsteth for thee, my flesh longeth for thee in a dry and thirsty land, where no water is; to see thy power and thy glory, so as I have seen thee in the sanctuary. Because thy loving-kindness is better than life, my lips shall praise thee" (Ps. 63:1-3).

God is an awesome and amazing God; He wants to build a close and loving relationship with His people. The connection between God and man that was lost at the beginning of creation is now restored as we come into His kingdom through Jesus Christ.

Additionally, God's foremost desire is that we should seek and do His will in everything we do.

"But the Comforter, which is the Holy Ghost, whom the Father will send in my name, he shall teach you all things, and bring all things to your remembrance, whatsoever I have said unto you" **(Jn. 14:26).**

The Holy Spirit is an efficient reminder, who helps us to seek God's will, thus making the relationship with our Creator stronger and more affectionate.

3. To gain wisdom

"Now we have received, not the spirit of the world, but the Spirit which is of God; that we might know the things that are freely given to us of God. Which things also we speak, not in the words which man's wisdom teacheth, but which the Holy Ghost teacheth; comparing spiritual things with spiritual" **(1 Cor. 2:12-13).**

Our wisdom is not worldly in nature, but supernatural and it gives us the knowledge and understanding of the mysteries of God. God's wisdom surpasses all knowledge and the world cannot partake in it, because it is a heavenly gift.

4. To gain peace with God

The mind of Christ keeps our hearts and gives us inner peace. It transforms us from within to the extent that even when the storm and hardship of life hit us, we stand firm on the solid Rock of Christ where the tides and billows cannot disturb us. Brethren, we are safe and secure in the hands of God, unaffected by the external changes caused by different circumstances of life.

"For to be carnally minded is death; but to be spiritually minded is life and peace"

(Rom. 8:6).

Truly, inner peace helps us to live peacefully with people around us. One of the basic proofs that God is present in any place or event is abundant peace. If God is truly there, peace must reign. A peaceful mind will rarely lack direction. *"And the peace of God, which passeth all understanding, shall keep your hearts and minds through Christ Jesus"* **(Phil. 4:7)**.

5. To distinguish between right and wrong

The mind of Christ is an excellent Spirit of judgment and discernment that empowers us to distinguish between good and evil.

"Give me understanding, and I shall keep thy law; yea, I shall observe it with my whole heart" **(Ps. 119:34)**.

There is no limit to the quality and quantity of discernment we receive when we begin to lead a life that imitates Christ. If we truly possess the mind of Christ, we would quickly identify sin and forsake things that would lead us astray or drive us away from His holiness.

6. Redemption from spiritual death

To be spiritually minded leads to life, but carnality will always lead to death.

"There is a way which seemeth right unto a man; but the end thereof are the ways of death" **(Prov. 14:12)**.

However, imitating Christ can keep us from this road of destruction. The mind of Christ will keep us from spiritual death and also give us abundant life. *"For to be carnally minded is death, but to be spiritually minded is life and peace"*

(Rom. 8:6).

A carnal mind grants an open invitation to sin and evil thoughts. If we consciously develop the mind of Christ in us through the Holy Spirit, we can live peaceful and holy lives.

"Therefore, brethren, we are debtors, not to the flesh, to live after the flesh. For if ye live after the flesh, ye shall die: but if ye through the Spirit do mortify the deeds of the body, ye shall live" **(Rom. 8:12-13).**

7. To please God

If we want to please God, it becomes imperative for us to have the mind of Christ. For without the mind of Christ, we cannot please God. Jesus Himself sought to completely please the Father in everything He did. For instance, when He was in the Garden of Gethsemane, the night before He was crucified He said, *"Father, if thou be willing, remove this cup from me: nevertheless, not my will, but thine, be done"* **(Lk. 22:42).**

He decided to please God and do His will, despite the humongous pain of crucifixion that hovered around Him.

"For I came down from heaven, not to do mine own will, but the will of him that sent me" **(Jn. 6:38).**

Realistically, Jesus' statement in John 8:29 must challenge every Christian to become more committed and devoted to pleasing God. Pleasing God is equal to doing His will. Moreover, walking according to His will includes keeping ourselves holy and free from the filth of sin. This is only possible with the presence and power of the Holy Spirit.

"I beseech you therefore, brethren, by the mercies of God, that you present your bodies a living sacrifice, holy, acceptable to God, which is your reasonable service" **(Rom. 12:1).**

Despite Satan's relentless attempts to distort the image of God in us through sin, Christ has come and saved us from the depravities of our fallen nature. He has turned to us His glorious face that reflects the light of God upon us. He has suffered the punishment of our sins. He has given us the authority to regain the likeness of God and to dwell in His presence till eternity. Praise the Lord!

CHAPTER 2

SATAN'S DISTRACTIVE STRATEGIES

Evidently, Satan is a crafty, tricky and foxy liar. He has cunningly programmed his demonic power to permeate the world in a way that we may not easily detect. He glamorizes sin and makes it look appealing on the surface. This is evident especially in the current age where art, recreation and even the most basic things like books or children's cartoons are tinged with satanic trademarks. He is slowly, but steadily digging his ugly claws into the hearts of people and colonizing them. Therefore, it is perfectly correct to call Satan the ruler of this world.

"Now is the judgment of this world: now shall the prince of this world be cast out" (**Jn. 12:31**).

Closely observe how the King of kings and the Lord of lords referred to the archenemy of man, not denying the fact that Satan has infiltrated His creation. Satan has established his own government in this world, and it would be an act of utter foolishness if we trivialize the destructive tendencies of this enemy.

It would only make us weaker and more susceptible to satanic attacks, while he becomes stronger. The most potent way of conquering the devil is to arm ourselves with knowledge and understanding of God's word like Jesus, and appropriately wield it against the devil.

Previously, we have beamed the searchlight of God's word on the operations of Satan, to know how he tried to usurp the authority of God by distorting His image in man. Having recorded a colossal failure in his attempt to overthrow the Kingdom of God, consequently, he has tweaked his plan and he is frantically working on how to colonize the world.

SATANIC MISSION

His agelong threefold objectives have not changed. He is bent on stealing our authority in Christ, luring us into eternal death through sin, and destroying the image of God that our Lord Jesus Christ purchased for us by His death and resurrection (see John 10:10).

Regardless of the schemes of Satan, God desires that we wholeheartedly put our trust in Him. God wants us to keep our gaze fixed on Him.

"Because he hath set his love upon me, therefore will I deliver him: I will set him on high, because he hath known my name. He shall call upon me, and I will answer him: I will be with him in trouble; I will deliver him, and honor him" **(Ps. 91:14-15)**.

Graciously, our God is nearer to us than we can ever imagine, and He is our present help in our time of need. Though the current age of Satanic Colonization is threatening, we serve a God who is too faithful and too powerful to fail. He will not leave or ignore us, and He has promised to be with us even to the end of the age.

DISTRACTION: THE ENEMY'S WEAPON OF CHOICE

One of the greatest tools employed by Satan is distraction. Therefore, it is no surprise that he aims at shifting our focus from God to ephemeral things. He knows that by focusing on the Almighty God, the source of sustainable peace and joy, His Spirit will order our steps and keep us away from sin, as well as destroy Satan's kingdom on earth.

Satan's primary weapon that grants him success in colonizing the world is distraction. Distraction is a doorway that leads to destruction. But in order to fully comprehend Satan's strategy, we must understand what distraction means and what are the possible ways of being distracted. This understanding will greatly help us to take up the full armor of God and tackle the fiery darts of distraction.

THE ANATOMY OF DISTRACTION

The Webster Dictionary defines distraction as something that diverts attention or a diversion. The term distraction may be synonymous with confusion, perplexity, disturbance, disorderliness. In the simplest words, distraction can be described as something that shifts your attention.

Satan often causes chaos, confusion, and disorderliness. The first confusion he created was when he craftily diverted Adam and Eve's attention from all other trees to the forbidden tree. Man was fully focused on God until Satan precipitated a devilish paradigm shift occasioned by introducing a new idea that contradicted God's command. Hence a road that diverges into two pathways lies ahead of every man; one leads to destruction and the other to everlasting life.

"There is a way which seemeth right unto a man; but the end thereof are the ways of death" (**Prov. 14:12**).

In his guile, Satan may make sin seem right and harmless, but sin is the surest path to death. Therefore, while the world vehemently debates and swims in the pool of confusion, asking which way leads to God, Jesus plainly dispels the confusion by saying, *"I am the way, the truth, and the life: no man cometh unto the Father, but by me"* (**Jn. 14:6**).

No confusion can stand the presence of God, because His glory gives and creates order where there is disorderliness and replaces confusion with clarity, tranquility, hope, and guidance.

After the fall, humanity lost the effortless ability to maintain their focus on God. Today, we live in an age of unprecedented distraction. We are constantly bombarded by media, technology and worldly things that distract us. This has conferred some negative effects on us, such as: shorter attention span, poor reading culture, and tardiness. Gradually, we are becoming conditioned to distraction as an acceptable way of life.

THE DANGERS OF DISTRACTION

The adverse impact of distraction while driving is one of the major causes of road accidents. For example, in the United States, it has been reported that people tend to read a text, chat or call while driving. Sometimes drivers are distracted by some objects on the side of the road and their attention is shifted from driving to looking, resulting often in ghastly accidents.

Spiritual distraction is similar but more dangerous. In a bid to make us lose focus, Satan hurls various distractions at us. Evidently, it is a battle that takes place in the mind. Have you observed how our minds wander in countless directions whenever we settle down to pray or study God's word?

Often, we are like distracted drivers that lose their focus on the road. Spiritual distraction takes our focus off God. When this happens, we lose control and stray into sin. By default, the fallen and selfish nature we inherited from our first parents is highly susceptible to distraction. Therefore, when we rely on our own strength, regardless of how well-meaning we are, we will fall, fail and faint.

"Now if I do that I would not, it is no more I that do it, but sin that dwelleth in me. I find then a law, that, when I would do good, evil is present with me" **(Rom. 7:20-21).**

Naturally, our flesh will rebel against the will of God. When we succumb to fleshly desires, sin immediately takes over. However, when we beam our focus on Jesus, He empowers us, and every distraction that produces fleshly desire fades away.

SUBTLE INVASION OF DISTRACTION

Basically, distraction involves shifting our attention from something or someone of greater importance to something or someone of lesser importance. This is exactly what Satan does when he distracts us. He attempts to shift our primary focus away from God and fixes it on other inconsequential things (gods or idols).

Craftily, Satan has rebranded idolatry and we are tempted to commit it (see Exodus 20:1). Gradually, we are replacing God with people or material things, thereby, sinning against God.

Today, Satan uses different types of distractions. He has subtly employed money, power, fame, pleasure, sex, technology and things like clothes, pieces of jewelry, cars, and others to shift our gaze from the author and finisher of our faith – Jesus Christ. Clearly, the media has successfully glamorized these things. Notice how sex and fame have permeated Hollywood; they prioritize self-pleasure over morality.

There are other seemingly harmless ways through which Satan distracts us in our personal lives. Sometimes, he plants doubt in our heads regarding our own capabilities. Consequently, we may begin to compare ourselves to others and forget the purpose for which God has created us. If care is not taken, Satan may keep us caught up by the web of unending chores or encompass us with bad company. At other times, Satan may lure us to gossip about other people.

All these things work intricately inside our minds. Surprisingly, Satan requires just a crevice to gain access into our lives and take over. Therefore, it becomes imperative to cling to God and vehemently resist the devil. Expectedly, the more engaged you are with God's word, the less prone to distraction you will be.

Another distraction that has gradually burrowed its way to the epicenter of the Church in recent years is the prosperity gospel. Undoubtedly, God has promised prosperity to His people; however, He does not want us to worship prosperity as an idol.

"Beloved, I wish above all things that thou mayest prosper and be in health, even as thy soul prospereth" **(3 Jn. 2)**.

The promise of physical prosperity comes after the prosperity of our souls. That is, when we have first sought the kingdom of God and His righteousness, God is committed to giving us material prosperity. Unfortunately, prosperity preachers are now equating earthly possessions to righteousness. Apostle Paul speaks of such pastors in Philippians 3:18-19: *"For many walk, of whom I have told you often, and now tell you even weeping, that they are the enemies of the cross of Christ: whose end is destruction, whose God is their belly, and whose glory is in their shame, who mind earthly things."*

Amazingly, Satan tried to distract Jesus, but he failed blatantly. Matthew Chapter 4 gives an account of Jesus being tempted by Satan in the wilderness. Cleverly, he quoted the Scriptures out of context, and attempted to distract Jesus from the Father's purpose for Him to the things of the world.

Satan quoted the Scriptures and veiled his schemes with the cloak of God's word. However, Jesus accurately replied with the Word of God without trying to give a second thought to Satan's evil plans. Jesus sets an example of how the sword of the Spirit (the Word of God) is the only weapon with which we can silence the serpent's tongue.

"Finally, my brethren, be strong in the Lord, and in the power of his might. Put on the whole armor of God, that ye may be able to stand against the wiles of the devil. For we wrestle not against flesh and blood, but against principalities, against powers, against the rulers of the darkness of this world, against spiritual wickedness in high places" **(Eph. 6:10-12)**.

There are several other biblical examples of people, whose lives were used to give a stern warning against distraction. Take Martha, Lazarus' sister, for example. In one of Jesus' visits to her home, Martha was engrossed with cooking, while Jesus was teaching. Mary, her sister, on the other hand, sat at the feet of the Lord Jesus, listening to His powerful teaching. After a while, Martha complained about the fact that she was not assisted by Mary. However, Jesus' response was instructive: *"Martha, Martha, thou art careful and troubled about many things: but one thing is needful; and Mary hath chosen that good part, which shall not be taken away from her"* (**Lk. 10:41-42**).

Mary was laser focused on Jesus, while Martha was engrossed with activities that have no eternal relevance. She was distracted by her responsibilities, which shifted her focus away from the precious Lamb of God. Consequently, she became anxious and frustrated. She was overwhelmed by the worry of how to serve the guests as well as do other chores. Jon Bloom said that "God is not nearly as interested in our efficiency as He is in our faith."

Truthfully, until Jesus addressed her, Martha did not recognize her source of distraction. Jesus made her realize that her priorities were misplaced. Often, when engrossed with activities, we fail to recognize how distracted we have become. We must continually probe and question ourselves to know if we are seeking the Person of higher importance or clinging to the things of lesser importance. King David knew the importance of getting one's priority right, hence, he says in Psalm 27:4: *"One thing I have desired of the Lord, that will I seek after: that I may dwell in the house of the Lord all the days of my life, to behold the beauty of the Lord, and to inquire in His temple."*

It is important we ask the following questions: do we desire God above other things? Is our treasure placed in heaven where moth and rust cannot destroy, or is it placed in this world, where they will be destroyed by moth and rust?

Another classic example we must learn from was the encounter that ensued between Jesus and Peter when they were at the Sea of Galilee (see Matthew 14:22-33). Peter was intrigued to see Jesus walking on water, then, Peter said to Him: *"Lord, if it is You, command me to come to You on the water."* Jesus agreed and commanded him to come. Immediately, Peter began to walk on water.

However, when the fierce wind blew, Peter became afraid and began to sink. This happened because he shifted his gaze away from Jesus and became distracted by the wind. Therefore, to keep ourselves from distractions, we must always focus our eyes on Jesus.

The Apostles of the early church had an unusual understanding of how to tame and manage distraction. Beloved, be informed, no spiritual height will exclude you from the temptations of distraction. However, your knowledge, insight, and understanding about God must be harnessed to manage distraction whenever it raises its ugly head.

"And in those days, when the number of the disciples was multiplied, there arose a murmuring of the Grecians against the Hebrews, because their widows were neglected in the daily ministration" **(Act 6:1).**

Assuredly, distraction will trail every form of growth, increase, promotion and accomplishment in your ministry, marriage, finance, career and other endeavors of life. At first, they look harmless and innocent, but when not tackled promptly, they have the tendency of taking the place of God, reducing Bible study time and ultimately, putting out the fire on our prayer altars.

"But we will give ourselves continually to prayer, and to the ministry of the word" (**Acts 6:4**).

Regardless of how successful you become, you must always be guarded by the resolution of the Apostles, because it takes continual prayer and diligent study of God's word to successfully conquer distractions.

Also, in our quest to gain mastery over distraction, we must carefully answer the following questions: what are those things distracting me in my walk with God? What makes my mind wander away whenever I sit to pray or meditate on God's word? What are those things hindering me from growing spiritually?

Truly, God wants us to be liberated from the captivity of distraction. He wants us to rise above its hurdles and walk with Him on the water where things are made possible by the mighty power of His Spirit.

Therefore, it is advisable not to ignore the pranks of the enemy and become careful of the ways he causes distraction to God's people.

"Be sober, be vigilant; because your adversary the devil, as a roaring lion, walketh about, seeking whom he may devour" (**1 Pet. 5:8**).

Satan is relentlessly working in numerous ways with the sole purpose of diverting our focus from our Lord Jesus Christ to mundane things. He wishes to distort God's image in us and wants us to fall into sin. The world we live in has been polluted with sin and distractions. Therefore, if we must be free from the shackles of distraction, our entire focus must beam at our resurrected Lord – Jesus Christ.

"Looking unto Jesus the author and finisher of our faith; who for the joy that was set before Him endured the cross, despising the shame, and is set down at the right hand of the throne of God" **(Heb. 12:2).**

It is the desire of God that we shun every distraction and solely focus on Him. He longs to be at the center of our lives, from waking up in the morning till sleeping at night. He wants us to set our minds meditating upon His word because His word is the only weapon that can destroy the enemy's schemes. He has commanded us to teach His word to our children and write it on the tablets of our hearts, just as He told the Israelites to hang it on their doorposts. This was aimed at keeping them focused on His word and holding fast to His law.

While Satan keeps pushing and distracting us, God's command remains: *"Be still, and know that I am God; I will be exalted among the nations, I will be exalted in the earth!"* **(Ps. 46:10).**

You must realize that God is not haphazard in His dealings with man, since He says be still, then, be still and know that He is in control.

Knowing Him is enough to break down the false image that Satan tries to put in our heads. When we know Him, we make Him the center of our attention. Therefore, we must stand firm and be still, listening to the quiet and gentle voice of the Spirit of God within us. No matter how hard Satan tries to establish his kingdom, he cannot succeed. Jesus has conquered him at Calvary. Satan operates by colonizing its victims. In fact, he is the one behind all forms of colonialisms that have occurred in history. Let us look at some of his techniques.

SOME COLONIALIST OPERATION TECHNIQUES

There is no doubt that colonialists operate in diverse ways. Some of their operations are conspicuous, while others are disguised. Besides, there are so many factors that determine the mode of colonialism experienced by an individual or group of people. Colonialists know the type of colonization that will be effective in a particular individual or in their selected region of operation.

HOW SATANIC COLONIALISTS OPERATE

Gaining freedom from the cruel grips of satanic colonialists begins with understanding their methods of operation. Surely, discernment is needed to direct every affair of our human endeavor and that includes our deliverance from satanic colonialists.

Therefore, I would like to expose some subtle but dangerous techniques used by colonialists to exploit and inhibit people from maximizing their potentials and fulfilling their purpose in life. This revelation is aimed at initiating freedom for all who have been held captive by satanic colonialists.

THEY ARE SUBTLE

"Now there arose up a new king over Egypt, which knew not Joseph. And he said unto his people, behold, the people of the children of Israel are more and mightier than we" (**Ex. 1:8-9**).

Amazingly, the cruelty of Pharaoh started with subtlety and later progressed to fierce persecution and infanticide. Although the children of Israel were God's own people, that didn't stop the evil effects of satanic subtlety from affecting them. Be informed: your spiritual status cannot exempt you from the subtle attempts of satanic colonialists, but discernment does.

Pathetically, from a soft and tender approach, Pharaoh's wickedness evolved and metamorphosed into a long period of servitude for the children of Israel. Often, this is the template used by Satan. He will disguise as a harmless entity, but eventually, he will steal, kill and destroy.

LIKE A RUSHING FLOOD

"When the enemy shall come in like a flood, the Spirit of the Lord shall lift up a standard against him" **(Is. 59:19).**

Satan and his cohorts understand the power of numbers. Satan knows that he cannot efficiently function alone. Remember, when he was to stage his rebellion in heaven against God, he subtly enticed other angels. Eventually, one-third of the heavenly Angels fell with him. Truly, Satan still engages this method of using the power of numbers to bring people under his control.

Be reminded, Daniel was not condemned until a group of people maligned his piety. In the days of Jehoshaphat, a great multitude of soldiers came against him – too many to number. Also, before the crucifixion of Jesus, a great number of people came under a satanic alliance to condemn Him.

God knows that satanic colonialists have learned this approach from Satan, hence, the word of God says, when the enemy shall come in like a flood, the Spirit of the Lord shall lift up a standard against him. Kindly note that even if a group of people support a particular wrong course, that doesn't make it right in the sight of God. Satan is an expert at recruiting a crowd; hence, your perspective about "majority carries the vote" must be decimated by divine wisdom.

THEY ARE EVIL SEED PLANTERS

"But while men slept, his enemy came and sowed tares among the wheat, and went his way" **(Matt. 13:25).**

Satanic colonialists often perpetuate their evil unnoticed because they are progressive in their approach. Be informed: satanic colonialists don't plant trees, they only plant seeds and eventually, their evil seeds will grow into evil trees.

This crafty approach of planting seeds, not trees, is the climax of subtlety. Be reminded: Delilah's seed to Samson was erotic love, but it grew into blindness and termination of a great ministry. Judas Iscariot's seed to Jesus was a hug, but it grew into betrayal and death.

Satanic colonialists understand the mystery of progression and continuity. Hence, they have designed TV shows, video games, recreation centers whose activities are aimed at damping your love for God. Do not forget that seeds are small and sometimes unnoticeable; this is the reason why you must fight every nonchalant attitude because it is the membrane that covers the satanic atomic bomb.

SUBSTITUTIONARY APPROACH

"And Jacob said, sell me this day thy birthright" **(Gen. 25:31).**

Satanic colonialists are eagle-eyed. Easily, they can spot gifts, talents, and graces in people, without wasting time.

Their mission is to craftily collect these lofty possessions and exchange them with ineptitude.

Interestingly, trade by barter is obsolete, but spiritual trade by barter is still in vogue. An example of how this plays out was the crafty approach employed by Jacob after Esau had gullibly sold his birthright.

Amazingly, this satanic approach was consistently seen all through Scripture; Potiphar's wife wanted to give Joseph a momentary satisfaction and rob him of his global relevance. Satan wanted to give Jesus mundane properties and strip Him of His Lordship. Pathetically, the young Prophet substituted his glorious vision with the blurred and forsaken vision of the Old Prophet. Consequently, he became lunch for a lion. Ordinary 30 shekels of silver erased the name of Judas Iscariot from the book of life. Beloved, you must watch the "substitutionary approach" of satanic colonialists.

Sincerely, the techniques of satanic colonialists discussed here are not exhaustive, but if you can pay attention to these commonly employed techniques already discussed, then, you have armed yourself with the appropriate ammunitions that will effectively destroy the operations of satanic colonialists.

EVILS OF SATANIC COLONIZATION

From the inception of the fall of Satan, he has never done one good thing. Disturbingly, a voice from heaven cursed the earth when Satan was banished from heaven. Every satanic activity and colonization is characterized by evil and pain. It becomes imperative to understand these evils in order to develop total disdain and hatred for them. A few of these evils will be expounded in this chapter.

"For strangers are risen up against me, and oppressors seek after my soul: they have not set God before them" **(Ps. 54:3).**

Satan doesn't give life; instead, he is an unrepentant killer. Have you noticed that death came immediately he successfully lured Eve? Everywhere Satan goes, death follows. His short but painful visit to Job's life occasioned an untold misery in his family, wealth, and health.

No wonder James 4:7 counsels us to resist the devil. Any time satanic colonialists are left unchallenged, their attacks are often destructive and catastrophic. King David ignored the wickedness of Absalom and it took the intervention of God to restore David's leadership. In your case, learn to discern and resist these enemies, and your victory will be absolute.

CAPTIVATION AND ENSLAVEMENT

Satanic colonialists inhibit their victims from enjoying any type of freedom. Therefore, it is not unusual for their victims to live their lives in pain, sickness, poverty, barrenness and various calamities.

Pharaoh exemplified the wickedness of satanic colonialists; forty-three decades of servitude were nothing to him. Despite God's instruction to him, he was stiff-necked, until his untimely destruction ended his reign. "Who is that God?" was his arrogant response.

Similarly, regardless of the pain and wasted time, satanic colonialists will not allow their victims to go.

THE PROLIFERATION OF UNGODLY BOOKS
AND CULTURAL INSTITUTIONS THAT ENDANGER BELIEVERS

Satanic colonialists are inventors of ungodly habits, activities, and devices. Their sole aim is to sway believers from the path of righteousness and victory. God knew this when He instructed Joshua to focus solely on the book of the law because safety, success, and victory are contained in it.

"This book of the law shall not depart out of thy mouth; but thou shalt meditate therein day and night, that thou mayest observe to do according to all that is written therein: for then thou shalt make thy way prosperous, and then thou shalt have good success" ***(Joshua 1:8)***.

In contemporary times, there is a subtle introduction of ungodly books, cartoons, religious practices, occultism, films, sports, and other activities. The Word of God has commanded all believers to flee from every appearance of evil.

CHAPTER 3

INTERNAL DISTRACTIONS – ANXIETY

Satan's foremost attempt to distract us always begins in our hearts. Just like he did to Adam and Eve, he has not changed his mode of attack; he will cunningly whisper into our hearts before his attempt to cause any internal or external chaos. The mind is the battleground of life. Certainly, victory is won or lost in the hearts of men.

Manipulation of the mind is a clever way of satanic attacks against the body of Christ because internal distraction enforced on an individual will gradually build up to a massive problem. Little by little, if this is not quickly controlled, it will spread in the body of Christ and quietly lead the whole Church towards destruction. Satan is an observant foe who is monitoring all our steps. He knows exactly when to attack or take advantage of our ignorance, carelessness, weaknesses, and frailties. Besides, he knows when to flee and remain on the defensive mode.

EFFECTS OF ANXIETY

Anxiety is one of the choicest weapons of Satan. Webster Dictionary defines anxiety as an "apprehensive uneasiness or nervousness usually over an impending or anticipated ill."

Medically, anxiety refers to "an abnormal and overwhelming sense of apprehension and fear often marked by physical signs (such as tension, sweating, and increased pulse rate), by doubt concerning the reality and nature of the threat, and by self-doubt about one's capacity to cope with it."

Anxiety is the troubling factor of life that shifts our minds from better things to the terrible ones and simultaneously worsens our mental condition as we permit its operation. It is based on self-destructiveness and bad anticipation of probable outcomes of the future.

Anxiety displays our inability to trust God's sovereignty, ability, and integrity. Regardless of how bad, unpleasant, fearful, terrible or hopeless the situation and circumstances seem to be; anxiety can never be the solution. Anxiety easily causes the memory of all the exceedingly great promises of God to sublime and evaporate from our hearts like a volatile substance. It frightens and makes us forget the assurance that Jesus gave us before His departure.

"These things I have spoken unto you, that in me ye might have peace. In the world ye shall have tribulation: but be of good cheer; I have overcome the world" **(Jn. 16:33).**

Medically, it has been concluded that anxiety is a mental condition that can shake or change people's personality, identity and as well distort their view and perception of the world.

It is a powerful weapon of the enemy. Although it is ignorantly ignored as an issue of mind, its titanic effect can manifest physical signs and symptoms. Realistically, it is an invisible force that produces visible results.

Over the years, the alarming rate of anxiety across the globe has compelled scientists to look into its soaring effect. Hence, they came up with drugs to treat it. Nevertheless, the world does not realize that it is a spiritual problem rather than a mere physical challenge. Therefore, it cannot be cured in a medical way; instead, it requires a spiritual remedy.

If anxiety is so rampant and unstoppable, what are the causes? Still, on this, how does it affect you? We need to dig deeper into this matter at hand, so that we may identify the strength and strategy of our archenemy and learn how to tackle it.

There are several kinds of disorderliness caused by different varieties of anxieties. Generally, these include social, separation or specific phobias. A person can have more than one anxiety disorder, which is a petrifying truth.

People with anxiety disorders may frequently have intense, excessive, persistent worry and fear about everyday situations.

Often, anxiety disorders involve repeated episodes of sudden feelings of intense anxiety and fear or terror that would reach a climax within minutes (panic attacks). This may cause them to live a relatively different life and to withdraw from social settings.

SIGNS AND SYMPTOMS OF ANXIETY:

- Tension, nervousness or restlessness
- A sense of imminent danger or panic
- Increased heart rate
- Rapid breathing (hyperventilation)
- Sweating

- Trembling
- Feeling weak or tired
- Trouble concentrating or thinking about anything other than the present worry (distraction)
- Insomnia

In life, physical or spiritual, there is no growth of any kind without fulfilling basic requirements or conditions. As a rule of thumb, anxiety is not excluded from these requirements. Often, there are various situations in people's lives that Satan uses to cause anxiety. We may be unaware of this truth; hence we tend to focus our attention on the surrounding situations and fail to see the steady impact of Satan in our lives. Anxiety is like a seed that Satan plants into our hearts and when it blooms, it leaves little room for God's word to stay in us. Remember, the fundamental ways of satanic operation are secret missions, hidden work, and encrypted ideology.

Still engulfed by ignorance, we get preoccupied with the worries of this life, and our worries weaken us internally and externally. Also, remember that Satan is not only seeking to torment us inwardly, but he is also desperately looking for a way to torture us outwardly, and this is what anxiety does to us.

Regardless of our age, gender, education, profession, race or nationality, there are situations that may trigger anxiety and as well establish it in our minds. They are common and unavoidable external conditions disturbing our inner peace. These may include:

- Stress at work or school
- Stress from personal relationships such as marriage or friends

- Stress from financial matters
- Stress from an emotional trauma such as the death of a loved one
- Stress from a serious medical illness that may tend to invade your life

It is good to note that the aforementioned adverse conditions do not start or develop overnight. Experience shows that through a gradual process of persistent lies that Satan sows into people's hearts, we may eventually begin to manifest physical illnesses and other associated effects. It is refreshing to know that Satan can only work from the outside because he cannot attack our new man – the regenerated spirit.

There is no doubt that Satan is aware of the fact that mounting a cluster of negative external circumstances around us will affect us internally. He is the ruler of this world and he uses adverse circumstances of life to trigger anxiety within us. Then he distorts our perception and we gradually begin to listen to his voice instead of the voice of the Holy Spirit.

"My sheep hear my voice, and I know them, and they follow me: And I give unto them eternal life; and they shall never perish, neither shall any man pluck them out of my hand" **(Jn. 10:27-28).**

Jesus clearly highlighted the difference between His children and the followers of Satan. Jesus referred to us as His sheep that know His voice and follow Him alone – not strangers. Being true followers of God, we should naturally recognize the voice of the Holy Spirit whenever He speaks to us.

Day by day, as we fellowship with the Holy Spirit, we become advanced in discernment. Therefore, we are able to recognize the voice of Satan and learn how to shun his suggestions whenever he speaks to us.

Our line of discernment is straight, simple and genuine. The Holy Spirit speaks in accordance with God's word while Satan only contradicts God's word. The voice of the Holy Spirit usually calms us down, even when we are surrounded by storms, whereas the voice of Satan only produces anxiety and fear, even amidst comfortable and peaceful circumstances.

In the New Testament, Jesus taught His disciples about anxiety; He commanded them never to worry about their lives, food, health, clothes or shelter. *"And he said unto his disciples, 'Therefore I say unto you, take no thought for your life, what ye shall eat; neither for the body, what ye shall put on. The life is more than meat, and the body is more than raiment. Consider the ravens: for they neither sow nor reap; which neither have storehouse nor barn; and God feedeth them: how much more are ye better than the fowls? And which of you with taking thought can add to his stature one cubit? If ye then be not able to do that thing which is least, why take ye thought for the rest? Consider the lilies how they grow: they toil not, they spin not; and yet I say unto you, that Solomon in all his glory was not arrayed like one of these. If then God so clothe the grass, which is today in the field, and tomorrow is cast into the oven; how much more will he clothe you, O ye of little faith? And seek not ye what ye shall eat, or what ye shall drink, neither be ye of doubtful mind. For all these things do the nations of the world seek after, and your Father knoweth that ye have need of these things. But rather seek ye the kingdom of God; and all these things shall be added unto you'"* **(Lk. 12:22-31).**

In this passage, Jesus teaches us not to worry about tomorrow. He reminds us that it is God who feeds all the birds of the air and clothes the lilies. Since we are more important than these, we should trust Him for all our needs. Therefore, we should not allow Satan to take over our mind and make us anxious.

He compares the flowers of the fields to Solomon and says that even Solomon was never as beautifully clothed as these plants. God is the One who gives beauty to flowers, even though they are short-lived.

Jesus sharply rebuked the disciples by exposing the littleness of their faith, He said, "O ye of little faith." This tells us that anxiety is the absence of faith. When there is anxiety, there is no place left for faith. However, to banish anxiety, you need to be filled with faith and you must believe that our God is Jehovah-Jireh: the God who provides. Our faith will grow as we saturate our hearts with the Word of God as instructed in Colossians 3:16: *Let the word of Christ dwell in you richly in all wisdom; teaching and admonishing one another in psalms and hymns and spiritual songs, singing with grace in your hearts to the Lord.*

God will provide everything in due time and will make all things beautiful in its season. You just have to keep your gaze on Him like Peter before he got distracted by the waves. God can kill, and he can make alive. He can build and as well destroy; He can protect and as well expose to danger. He is higher than the highest, the Alpha and Omega, the First and the Last, the beginning and the end. You should always remember that God has power over everything in life, either visible or invisible. He has the final say. Our sole responsibility is to seek God and involve Him in everything we do or need.

HOW TO OVERCOME ANXIETY

"Be careful for nothing; but in every thing by prayer and supplication with thanksgiving let your requests be made known unto God" **(Phil. 4:6).**

Apostle Paul presents to us various ways of controlling anxiety. According to him, prayer is foremost in handling anxiety. Prayer keeps our faith strong in God and keeps us focused on Him. We come in close fellowship with Him and equally build a shield against the wiles of the devil through a consistent prayer life.

Overcoming anxiety is one of the reasons why the Bible admonishes us to pray without ceasing (see 1 Thessalonians 5:17). This involves a continuous state of communion with the Holy Spirit, meditating on the Scriptures, memorizing and sharing them with others. Persistent prayer life is so driven by God's love and purpose that any kind of anxiety-causing distraction will not be able to gain access to the mind.

Compactly, the simple remedy to anxiety is: don't fix your eyes on the visible; you should rather focus on God.

"While we look not at the things which are seen, but at the things which are not seen: for the things which are seen are temporal; but the things which are not seen are eternal" **(2 Cor. 4:18).**

Any time you are anxious or frightened, you should quickly remember that you have shifted your gaze from the invisible God to the visible world. Obviously, leaving God out of the picture is dangerous and detrimental.

Truly, we fear and worry about ephemeral things, while we neglect the glorious hope that we have in the Lord Jesus

Christ. Instead, we need to keep our eyes on the eternal God, who is our refuge. He knows our future and also has unfathomable plans for us.

"Eye hath not seen, nor ear heard, neither have entered into the heart of man, the things which God hath prepared for them that love him" **(1 Cor. 2:9).**

You need not worry about the future or about current circumstances. God will safely preserve you through the situation. Provided you abide in God, the future will definitely birth amazing and jaw-dropping results because everything has been commanded by God to work together for your good. Every stubborn situation will ultimately bow in obedience to God's command.

You must always retain the truth in your heart that God is only found in the present and that the future lies in the palm of His hand. Besides, you should also learn that each day is a gift from God. Therefore, you ought to live each day at a time without yielding to the temptation of habitual anxiety that Satan hurls at us.

"Sufficient unto the day is the evil thereof" **(Matt. 6:34).**

The future belongs to God; He is wise and powerful enough to handle it. Yesterday is past and you should allow it to remain as past. It is irreparable and you cannot retrieve it. You should not bother yourself about it. Instead, focus your attention on God and what He is doing in your life today and be thankful for it.

While the world seeks refuge and solace in medicine and mental exercise to get rid of anxiety, we have full hope and assurance that God is by our side. Whatever form of anxiety that is threatening us, God is the surest solution. His Word is our armor against Satan's destructive lies. As Jesus used the Word of God in Matthew chapter four, when He was tempted by Satan after forty days of fasting and prayer, we too must use the Word of God whenever Satan launches his attack against us. Equipping ourselves with God's word and ceaseless prayer draw us closer to God, and where the Spirit of God is, there is freedom from anxiety. In His glorious light, anxieties vanish.

Scripturally, whatever occupies your mind becomes your god. Similarly, if anxiety is indulged, it will definitely become an idol. If you naively allow it to evolve to a giant like Goliath, it will stand in the way of your peace.

Regardless of the magnitude of anxiety hovering over your life, let the Holy Spirit comfort you with the soothing Word of God. There is no doubt that there are numerous things to worry about in life, but one thing is sure: none of them must separate you from God's love that is rooted in Christ Jesus. Refuse to focus on problems. Rather, stay focused on God, who is the universal solution. His love is excellent and eternal. Undoubtedly, that is all we need.

"For I am persuaded that neither death nor life, nor angels nor principalities nor powers, nor things present nor things to come, nor height nor depth, nor any other created thing, shall be able to separate us from the love of God which is in Christ Jesus our Lord" (**Rom. 8:38-39**).

DANIEL — THE SUPERHERO
_____

When you are in a tough situation, simply focus your attention on God and equally recall how He graciously dealt with people of old. A perfect example of a hero to recall and emulate is Daniel, who was thrown into the den of lions.

"My God hath sent His Angel, and hath shut the lions' mouths, that they have not hurt me: forasmuch as before Him innocence was found in me and also before thee, O King, have I done no hurt" **(Dan. 6:22).**

Although he was maliciously offered as food for hungry lions, he remained unharmed and the wild lions were miraculously made his pets and consequently became his emotional support animals. He remained focused on God, entrusting His life and security to Him. He was not perturbed or anxious. Rather, he was calm and joyful, because he knew that God would rescue him. Similarly, you too must trust God when anxiety strikes or when a situation tenses up, believing that God will never fail you. It is plainly written in the Bible that the devil goes about roaring like a lion, constantly seeking whom to devour. You need to be firm in your heart whenever lion-like situations stand to confront you; they cannot eat you up, because the God of Daniel is your God.

"Ye are of God, little children, and have overcome them: because greater is He that is in you than he that is in the world" **(1 Jn. 4:4).**

HIDDEN SECRETS OF TRIUMPH

It is evident that God is above all things, including human problems like sickness, lack, sorrow, pain, disappointments, and the heavy burdens of this everchanging world. Apparently, when you focus on God, He will lift you above your circumstances and give you His rest that descends on you like dew from the heavenly realms.

Instead of being overwhelmed by your burdens, let those burdens carry you to your breakthrough. Be on top of your challenges and not under them as promised in Deuteronomy 28:13: *"And the LORD shall make thee the head, and not the tail; and thou shalt be above only, and thou shalt not be beneath; if that thou hearken unto the commandments of the LORD thy God, which I command thee this day, to observe and to do them."*

Let the Word of God dwell in you richly in all wisdom and follow its dependable path to your breakthrough. This is the way of peace, living in the light of God's presence. Typical examples of people who refused to carry their burdens but made those burdens carry them were the lepers in the Old Testament. The society banished them to an isolated part of the city, but their condition drove them to uncover a prompt and permanent solution to the ravaging famine.

"Then they said one to another, we do not well; this day is a day of good tidings, and we hold our peace. If we tarry till the morning light, some mischief will come upon us: now therefore come, that we may go and tell the king's household" (**2 Kings 7:9**).

There will always be problems in this fallen world, but we are to focus our utmost attention on the risen Lord – who has conquered the world.

"Thou wilt show me the path of life: in thy presence is fulness of joy; at thy right hand there are pleasures for evermore" (**Ps. 16:11**).

Learn to always bask in the love of our Lord. As His face shines upon us, He will bless us with His peace. He will gradually guide us to the right destination, and we don't need to be anxious about the future.

Instead of allowing problems to weigh you down, climb on top of them and use them as reminders to rededicate, reconnect and refocus your life on God. Consequently, He will fill you with His presence, love, and incomparable peace. These invisible realities are available for you anywhere, at any time, and they will jointly grant you irreplaceable joy.

There is an absolute need to carefully keep pace with God; you can't be faster than God and still enjoy His blessings. This is the only way to enjoy abundant life brought to us by our Lord and Savior. A life of total dependency on God is full of peace, joy, love and rest. Factually, as you focus on Him, you will be clothed with His light and no darkness will be able to overcome you.

"I am the light of the world; he that followeth me shall not walk in darkness, but shall have the light of life" (**Jn. 8:12**).

Generally, the forces of darkness are the source of inhibiting weights trying to pull you down. But when the light of God floods your heart, darkness will disappear, because darkness is merely the absence of light. So, keep your gaze on Him: the Light of the world. Let Him shine the light of the knowledge of His glory upon you.

Instead of worrying about what is ahead of you in the future, glue your eyes on God and He will take care of everything that pertains to you. Over and above your thought, His power will flow freely into your life through the spiritual cord that connects you to Him. If you maintain this state, you will no longer feel inadequate, because His all-sufficient graces will envelop you. Expectedly, as you live in the radiance of God's presence, His peace will reign and rain upon you.

"Teaching them to observe all things whatsoever I have commanded you: and, lo, I am with you always, even unto the end of the world" (**Matt. 28:20**).

Standing on this promise is not negotiable, because it is explicitly stated that God is always present with us during the thick and thin of life. No one can truly understand the state of your mind, but Jesus does. While Satan continues in his business of laying distractions in the way of believers, Jesus Himself will be with you to comfort, inspire, encourage and sustain you through it all.

CHAPTER 4

INTERNAL DISTRACTIONS – FEAR

In all circumstances of life, we either operate by faith or by fear. Fear is a veritable weapon used by the devil to distract us from God and His will. The believer's greatest enemy, Satan, often plants needless fear in our hearts in order to prevent us from living lives of faith. This enemy is recording success after success by turning almost everything to an object of fear in the minds of people. For instance, fear of the unknown, criticism, rejection, failure, sickness, accident, robbery, attacks, natural disaster, the death of a loved one, and ultimately the fear of people in authority, have become a major issue in our spiritual and physical lives. Unknown to God's people, Satan is using all these as obstacles to prevent us from doing what God has called us to do. Therefore, although we profess to be strong believers, we tend to confine ourselves within our little shells of pseudo-security and peace.

Apparently, it is a common disease among us to assume and sometimes accept failure before we even attempt to step out in faith to face our challenges and overcome the forces of setbacks. More often than not, most of us may not even know why we fear a particular thing. This is because our concern and fear may stem from a previous mishap or a horrible incidence that happened in the past. The memory might have faded away, but the fear lingers on in our subconscious mind, and this is how the enemy cunningly works in our lives.

He quietly analyzes our behaviors and uses life's circumstances to hold us back from future progress. Therefore, there is a likelihood that most of the things we dread happened to us in the past or we have witnessed them in the lives of other people. However, there is no established rule that the evil experience of other people must happen to us.

In the previous chapter, we learned about the internal strategy of anxiety and how it disrupts the thought process of people in order to keep them from relying on God's promises and power. In the same vein, this chapter will focus on fear, which is another powerful weapon that the enemy is using to militate against people from within. Over time, the seed of fear planted by Satan takes roots in our minds in such a way that it may become so difficult to uproot them. However, the Word of God affirms that: *"There is no fear in love; but perfect love casteth out fear: because fear hath torment. He that feareth is not made perfect in love"* (**1 Jn. 4:18**).

God's love perfects, upholds and redeems us from internal attacks of the enemy. Although, we are constantly surrounded by unpredictable changes, decay, disintegration, and trepidation, we have a God, who is the same yesterday, today, and forever. He will drive away any fear that may invade your life, if only you allow His love to fill your heart.

It becomes imperative to have a full grasp of how to curb the monster called fear, how it can affect us and the ability of God's word to root it out completely.

Webster Dictionary defines fear as: "an unpleasant often strong emotion caused by anticipation or awareness of danger." This unpleasant feeling comes into our hearts before taking its place. According to statistics obtained from the U.S. National Institute of Mental Health on 4th of September 2016, the percentage of dreaded things that will never take place is 60%; the percentage of things feared that are considered to be insignificant for you is 90%; and the percentage of health-related fear that will never happen is 88%. So, what is the basis of fear if the chance of its occurrence or manifestation is extremely low? President Roosevelt said, "The only thing we have to fear is fear itself." This is true because fear is a seed that grows up and spreads its branches into bigger and more sinister terrors. Therefore, the tree must be chopped at its roots.

It is unsurprising that *"Do not fear"* is the most repeated command in the Bible.

"Fear thou not; for I am with thee. Be not dismayed, for I am thy God. I will strengthen thee; yea, I will help thee. Yea, I will uphold thee with the right hand of my righteousness **(Is. 41:10).**

This portion of the Bible is an example of God's constant reminder to Israel not to permit fear in their hearts. The emphatic repetitions of God's command against fear are followed by God's promises and confession of love for His people.

Interestingly, God did not only instruct us to live a life devoid of fear, but He also promised us His ever-abiding presence and faithfulness. Hence, we have the assurance that we are not alone. He is present with us at all times and has control over all circumstances of life. It is not strange that Satan might remind and as well threaten us through the sprouting seed of fear in our hearts. However, God has demonstrated His love towards us by promising to help, strengthen and uphold us with His right hand of righteousness.

Typically, different things may trigger fear in our hearts, but only the three prominent types of fear will be considered.

PROTECTIVE FEAR

Not every kind of fear is bad. Protective fear is the one that helps us respond cautiously to a dangerous situation. It is a kind of defense mechanism that is beneficial to us. For example, parents often instruct their children to carefully look at both sides of the road before crossing, to avoid an accident. Often, we would say, "Don't keep your hand on the stove or you will get burnt." These are examples of protective fear, which are essential to be inculcated into our minds in order to prevent hazardous situations as well as react wisely when we have a similar encounter.

GODLY FEAR

"The fear of the Lord is clean, enduring for ever; the judgments of the Lord are true and righteous altogether" **(Ps. 19:9).**

Godly fear is only found in the heart of believers. This is the reverence we have towards God, which subsequently compels us to refrain from sin and its consequences. Scripturally, "Fear the Lord" means to acknowledge, revere and submit to Him for who He is. To fear God does not mean to be terrified of God, but to respect and reverence God. This type of fear is another example of a good type of fear. Certainly, without godly fear, we will be wallowing in sin and have no respect for God and His commandments.

"The fear of the Lord is the beginning of wisdom and the knowledge of the Holy is understanding" (**Prov. 9:10**).

CHRONIC FEAR

In comparison to protective and godly fear, chronic fear is an unhealthy form of fear and must be totally avoided. It is the type of fear that Satan uses as his weapon and is intended to destabilize the lives of God's people.

Usually, chronic fear will either start as a result of sin or it may arise out of certain negative experiences and assumptions. When it persists, it turns into anxiety, stress, and depression, and could develop into suicidal tendencies. This fear prevents people from doing what God called them to do and is predominantly based on personal assumptions.

However, negative fear is capable of affecting us adversely in different forms. Evidently, if fear is not controlled, it may become destructive.

Here are some negative resultant effects of chronic fear.

FEAR BRINGS TORMENT

Torment is one of the effects of chronic fear. It is the forerunner of Satan and a faithful servant of destruction. If Satan could successfully inject fear into your mind, that may, in turn, affect your physical health. It is apparent that any prolonged mental pain results in physical agony.

"There is no fear in love; but perfect love casteth out fear: because fear hath torment. He that feareth is not made perfect in love" **(1 Jn. 4:18).**

God's love is pure and perfect; if He could save us from the torment and horror of hell, then He is able to redeem us from fear and all its effects.

Fear has the potential to restrain; fear will restrain you from doing God's will if you are not careful about it. It will limit your abilities and ultimately stop you from stepping out of your comfort zone. Furthermore, it will prevent you from using your talents for the glory of God. It will make you unproductive by constantly reminding you of your past failures so that you will be discouraged from making any other attempt.

An example of this is when God told Gideon to reset and reselect his chosen men. Without argument, fear instantly turned the chosen to unqualified, able men to disabled and gladiators to spectators.

"Now therefore go to, proclaim in the ears of the people, saying, whosoever is fearful and afraid, let him return and depart early from mount Gilead..." **(Judg. 7:3).**

God knows that fear cannot take you any further towards your purpose and will always hold you back. Therefore, He commanded the people to make an irrevocable choice between fear and faith, victimization and victory. Painfully, in one day, twenty-two thousand soldiers (armed men of God) returned (to the paralytic camp of fear), and only ten thousand people remained in the assailing and victorious camp of faith.

FEAR IS A ROBBER

Sometimes fear changes the outcome of our endeavors. Despite God's blessings conferred on us, fear may just keep us away from what is already ours in Christ. An example of this is when Peter walked on water towards Jesus. He was able to walk as long as He had his gaze fixed on Jesus. However, when he allowed fear to interfere, he began to sink. Isn't it true that we demonstrate similar attitudes in our personal lives? We tend to replace faith with fear and that could result in negativity and failure.

Job was a man greatly blessed by God, but when he stepped out of faith, he tasted the other side of life.

"For the thing which I greatly feared is come upon me, and that which I was afraid of is come unto me" (**Job 3:25**).

IT IS CONTAGIOUS

Fear is an invisible entity that can spread rapidly like an epidemic disease from one person to another.

"And the officers shall speak further unto the people, and they shall say, what man is there that is fearful and faint-hearted? Let him go and return unto his house, lest his brethren's heart faint as well as his heart" (**Deut. 20:8**).

Joshua and Caleb were superheroes that distinguished themselves from the midst of fear-infected spies sent to Canaan.

"Forty years old was I when Moses the servant of the Lord sent me from Kadeshbarnea to espy out the land; and I brought him word again as it was in mine heart. Nevertheless my brethren that went up with me made the heart of the people melt: but I wholly followed the Lord my God" (**Josh. 14:7-8**).

These examples from the Bible clearly show how we could transfer our fear to other people. They might not have personally witnessed the consequences of a situation, but our testimony is enough to plant faith or fear in their inward parts.

Therefore, as genuine believers, we must not allow fear to shift us from our vantage position and true identity.

"For God has not given us a spirit of fear, but of power and of love and of a sound mind" **(2 Tim. 1:7).**

Evidently, as we receive God's Spirit, the love of God becomes perfected in us. Since perfect love casts away fears, our fear will vanish, and we will begin to live a life of love and power. Indeed, all we need to do is to call out to God for help in our struggles and He will show up for us because according to Psalms 46:1 He is a very present help in times of trouble.

"I sought the Lord, and He heard me, and delivered me from all my fears" **(Ps.34:4).**

Above all, the key to overcoming fear is not any external motivation or the right use of your physical and mental strength. Instead, the surest antidote to fear is total reliance on God and His Word. Allow Him to take full charge as He promised not to leave nor forsake you. Keep your focus on Him like Daniel and be rest assured that He is with you even till the close of the age.

"But now thus saith the Lord that created thee, O Jacob, and he that formed thee, O Israel, fear not: for I have redeemed thee, I have called thee by thy name; thou art mine. When thou passest through the waters, I will be with thee; and through the

rivers, they shall not overflow thee: when thou walkest through the fire, thou shalt not be burned; neither shall the flame kindle upon thee" **(Is. 43:1-2).**

God has not promised us a life that is free from hardships, troubles, and distractions. However, He promised to be with us. He affirmed that while we are passing through the deepest water or hottest fire, we shall come out unharmed and unscathed, because of His presence that is with us.

Satan may make uncountable attempts to frighten us through chaotic circumstances of this world; he may even cause pain and as well as spur terror around us, but we know that in the end we shall not be consumed, because we are rooted in God's love and no one can pluck us out of the hollow of His hands. *"For I am persuaded that neither death nor life, nor angels nor principalities nor powers, nor things present nor things to come, nor height nor depth, nor any other created thing, shall be able to separate us from the love of God which is in Christ Jesus our Lord"* **(Rom. 8:38-39).**

CHAPTER 5

MODERN DISTRACTIONS – TECHNOLOGY

Since the second half of the 20th century, there has been a rapid life-transforming shift due to the widespread impact of the digital revolution. It has resulted in socialization on a large and widening scale which has transformed the lifestyle of every single person on earth.

The dawn of the Internet era has been a total game changer as multitudes have stepped out of the analog life into a digitalized universe. This pixelated world has rooted itself in our lives to such an extent that it seems inescapable. It has overtaken every area of life and its speed of advancement is truly amazing. It has not just connected people and built bridges to promote communication but has played an effective role in educating and transmitting information and knowledge to people from every nation of the world.

Furthermore, technology has enabled us to use better and faster tools, making us more productive and efficient without demanding a lot of time from us. We can literally complete certain tasks quicker than ever, such as sending messages, cooking or even cleaning the house. What is more spectacular is that there are constant efforts to create better and faster technologies than the current ones. As a result, our future is expected to be more advanced than what is currently obtainable.

However, there are monstrous facets of technology. While these technological advancements have brought appreciable ease and comfort, there is no denying that this digital revolution has intruded the privacy of people, making it difficult to detach personal lives from professional lives. People have integrated every aspect of their lives with digitalization as in the case of social media, hence, their personal responsibilities seem to hold lesser importance than previous years.

Additionally, there are several other issues that have popped up because of technology. It has created a fundamental shift which has brought us several advantages and disadvantages at the same time. As a result, those disadvantages pose a major threat to our spirituality by shifting our focus from God to other things. Today, most people are disturbingly engrossed with the technological devices that they miss out on precious real-life moments. They tend to seek validation and compete with people who in reality have to face similar challenges like them. It seems like people are running away from life's challenges and finding refuge in an undependable digital fortress.

Surprisingly, what is currently happening is not something that is unexpected. This present age is actually a fulfillment of the Word of God in Daniel 12:4 which says, *"But thou, O Daniel, shut up the words, and seal the book, even to the time of the end: many shall run to and fro, and knowledge shall be increased."*

People are preoccupied and caught up with worldly worries and unending challenges of life. Knowledge and information have exploded, but people have become emotionally and mentally crippled because they seemingly have everything at their disposal. They have lost patience and in turn, they seek faster results for their efforts.

In some cases, they may not even be willing to put any effort into work because of how technology has influenced their habits. They are now accustomed to comfort and their minds and bodies have adapted to it.

Therefore, the advent of technology has brought a fundamental shift in our culture. Our lifestyles have been radically overturned by the proliferation of technological gadgets. And so, the blessings and burdens of technology still continue to work their way into every nook and cranny of life as scientists take a more daring technological leap into the future.

Research over the last 20 years has shown that our brains, including those of our young children, are being reprogrammed by technology. Amazingly, there are currently 2.32 billion smartphone users in the world. This number is expected to increase to over 3 billion by 2022. Needless to say, Americans spend an average of eight hours every day staring at their devices. Out of those aged 18-24, 75% said they check their phones before they get out of bed. Once out of bed, Americans check their phones once every 4.3 minutes, or 221 times a day.

In all honesty, we are victims of technology in some ways or the other. Do you recall what the world looked like before the advent of technological plague? Evidently, some of you happened to have been born in a time when it was already too late, and digitalization had already started. Nevertheless, this was bound to happen, because the Word of God already prophesied it.

However, the current struggle is how to tackle these modern distractions. How can we possibly keep ourselves untouched and unpolluted by the world?

THE EVOLVING TECHNO-DISTRACTIONS

In this chapter, our searchlight will beam largely on the major distraction that Satan uses which is technology. We may not notice it, but in all his attempts to colonize the world, he has sabotaged our precious and irreplaceable asset: time, which ought to be invested in godly pursuit like spending time in fellowship with God, instead of wasting it on technology.

Technology in itself is not a bad thing. In fact, it is a blessing of God that emanated from the wisdom and intelligence that God granted to man. It helps us to communicate better by e-mail, telephone, and social media.

Television allows us to know what is going on in real time in any part of the world. We can FaceTime or Skype relatives and friends who are far away from us. Various mobile applications help us organize our daily lives. Facilities such as online banking and online shopping also save time and money, while Google maps help us get to places we want to go without stopping at gas stations to ask for directions. In addition to its merit, technology has also helped to spread the Gospel of Jesus Christ across the world. Globally, it has made the Holy Bible more accessible. We are experiencing more than 100 years of progress in the 21st century; it seemingly feels like 20,000 years of advancement. If we carefully observe the past few years, obviously, there are profound, astounding and rapid changes in our world.

While technology transforms our lives for the better, it also has its downside. Undoubtedly, it has the tendency of making us become lazier, less communicative with our loved ones, less attentive to details, indifferent to happenings in our surroundings, and to dwindling concentration span and decreased natural capacity to carry out tasks.

Besides, there are certain spiritual implications of excessive adoption, usage, and reliance on technology. It becomes imperative to look at the demerits of technology more closely and also ponder upon our own lives to see how technology has distorted our minds and clouded our perceptions.

We have lost the art of meditation; technology has adverse effects on a healthy soul and spirit. Having a soul that is at peace and in deep communion with God requires space, quietness, stillness, tranquility, and Selah (meaning pause). We need all these to hear the "still small voice" of Jehovah that will instruct and teach us the right path to follow. This issue has enormous implications on our ability to be with God, know Him personally and enjoy His presence. Psalm 46:10 might be the biggest indictment for Christ-followers in the 21st century: *"Be still and know that I am God."*

Painfully, we are no longer able to hear God's voice, because our minds are often preoccupied with distractions and worries of life. Even for entertainment and escape from problems, we tend to seek peace in technological devices. What we fail to recognize is that all of these gadgets compete to steal every moment of time and attention in our lives.

No wonder, we have trouble with prayer, solitude, silence, and meditation. Many marriages are breaking down and our youths are becoming more and more morally delinquent. This is because we are experts at maximizing technology, but inefficient at managing it. We are good at leveraging on technology, but not so good at limiting its excesses.

The next time you ride on a bus, a shuttle or take a flight, look at all the passengers around you and you will most likely find everyone's head buried in their devices. It is tragic how it has become an addiction!

We are exposed to uncontrollable risks and dangers; there is another worrisome side of technology. It is used by sexual predators, scam artists and terrorists to carry out their evil deeds. These have caused major heartaches around the world, including murders, broken relationships, huge financial losses, and spiritual backsliding. While technology is usually glorified and praised for its benefits, you will seldom find these dark sides being discussed. In fact, even if someone identifies these dangers, people ignore the warnings and continue to indulge in these sinful practices.

Technology has also caused psychological problems such as anxiety and depression. Constantly reeling after the happenings around the world can cause anxiety and several other disorders. They plant fear in your mind as you come to know the horrific incidences taking place around the world. You tend to keep your eyes on the worries of the world, which robs you of your peace. Another danger associated with the Internet that has become more prominent over the years is cyberbullying. This has given rise to societal pressure, insecurities and psychological disorders or in worse cases, suicide. Clearly, Satan is using all these subtle strategies to keep our minds from being focused on God. He keeps them troubled by the chaos around us instead of leading a prayerful life.

Our communication with God is distracted; uncontrolled technological consumption distracts us from reading the Bible. We have an increasingly hard time focusing on what we are reading when the telephone keeps ringing, text messages keep clicking, and notifications keep popping up on our mobile devices. We reflexively reach out for our phones every time, including in the church after every few seconds!

Yet, the Lord commanded in Joshua 1:8 that, "This Book of the Law shall not depart from your mouth; but you shall meditate on it day and night, that you may observe to do according to all that is written in it. For then you will make your way prosperous, and then you will have good success."

Despite God's command, we have so much occupied ourselves with technology that we no longer meditate on His Word. Probably, we don't even remember it after studying, because of the flow of information constantly being fed into our brains as we scroll through our phone screens.

We have lost the art of meditation due to techno-distractions. This is spiritually unhealthy! Have you noticed that the Bible references that we used to know off the top of our caps are no longer there? This is because we are so dependent on checking them up online that we do not open our Bibles to look it up ourselves, which would have helped us in memorizing and remembering them.

Our family relationships are negatively impacted. How about distraction to family conversations and relationships with people? When we are supposed to be connecting and bonding face-to-face with our family members, we are distracted and focused on our technological devices—whatever they may be. We are distracted by every new text message. We no longer prioritize the person by engaging in meaningful conversations and spending quality time with family and friends. Instead, we prioritize technology and escape reality for a virtual world. We get distracted by the person who is not there and neglect the one who is present with us.

In addition, instead of speaking face-to-face at home, technology has become the mode of communication even under the same roof. We are guilty of texting our siblings or family members while they are in the same place just because we are too lazy to get up and talk to them or do certain things on our own. This is keeping us from valuing and appreciating each other's presence. We talk to people who are not there and miss out on crucial facial expressions that help us understand one another's feelings and needs. This has become so common that it is difficult to imagine that we will ever abandon these habits. However, we can only pray that the Lord may deliver us all!

We are totally distracted and have accepted distraction as a modern culture. Truthfully, it is increasingly difficult to focus, pay attention for a long time, be actively involved in a conversation, have undistracted thoughts, pray, read, enjoy a quiet drive or be alone with ourselves and God.

Publilius Syrus said, *"To do two things at once is to do neither."* But our constant connection to our techno-gadgets also affects our abilities to work effectively. Recent studies of office workers revealed that people constantly stop what they are doing to read and respond to incoming emails. It is not unusual for them to glance at their inbox 30-40 times an hour. Does that sound familiar?

Multiple studies have proven that multi-tasking actually makes us less productive. In many respects, uncontrolled engagement with technology is not good for us. Thus, we need to urgently tackle these distractions from Satan.

His objective is to engross us with techno-activities to the extent that we may no longer listen to God's word or walk in His way. We must remember that we are not of this world; therefore, our conduct must be different from worldly people.

"A prudent man foreseeth the evil, and hideth himself: but the simple pass on, and are punished" **(Prov. 22:3).**

According to this verse, there are two characteristics that qualify an individual as smart, sensible and wise. First, they can discern paths that lead to trouble. They can foresee it before it even arrives. Smart people are not naïve. They don't go about looking for trouble, but they are on the lookout for danger and they have the ability to see it from a safe distance. They are always alert and on guard and they know how destructive the consequences of evil are.

In contrast, the simpleton, that is, the one who lacks good judgment, walks in blindly. Such people are not necessarily evil, sinful or immoral; they are just foolish and lack good judgment. They walk into situations that could have been avoided, but they fail to see the warning signs and just walk straight into the problem, thereby, inviting unnecessary trouble upon themselves.

Secondly, this Bible passage teaches us that a wise person would discern and avoid trouble. He makes the necessary adjustment to get out of the way of trouble. He "hides" himself, so that the trouble may not cause any harm to him. On the other hand, the foolish man is punished for his carelessness, recklessness, and foolishness. He is not just contemptible in God's sight, but his own actions punish him with several destructive consequences.

Beloved, nobody gets points for only seeing the trouble coming. The points are earned when trouble is wisely avoided. Often, we fail to discern trouble; hence, we simply pass on into them.

It is high time we begin to live our lives circumspectly, thereby, glorifying God with them. The Lord has shown us some of the dangers of technology to our souls, families, and relationship with God. We must ask ourselves whether we are just discerning the incoming trouble of techno-devices or earning points by avoiding them.

Therefore, the greatest fear in today's age is that we may lose our purpose and shift our focus from God because we mostly have our heads buried in our smartphones, iPads and other techno-gadgets. Consequently, we are missing out on some of the special moments that God planned for us. Also, we are missing the chance to communicate with and honor our spouses, play with our children and grandchildren, care for someone in our community or church, or observe an amazing sunset.

Today, take a wide and clear glance at your life and observe some technodangers God has opened your eyes to discern as distractions to your relationship with God, family, church or even to yourself. Identify them and pray over them. There is no challenge or problem in our lives that we cannot overcome if God is by our side.

It is advisable that we pray to God to help us fix our eyes on Him and keep walking with Him. We must ask God to deliver us from all of these distractions as well as help us to discipline our appetite for technology before it totally distracts us.

The key is to create a balance between all of life's blessings. Too much of anything is harmful to our spiritual and physical lives.

Below is a short but important prayer, which I encourage you to intensely pray in your secret place. May you learn to practice self-control and patience as you allow God to take over every aspect of your life, thereby, breaking loose from the grip of technological distraction in Jesus' name.

TECHNO-DELIVERANCE PRAYER

Dear Heavenly Father, I confess that I have allowed uncontrolled adoption and usage of technology to distract me, and thus interfere with my soul, relationships and work. I have given in to the strategies of Satan both intentionally and unintentionally. Lord, I humbly ask for forgiveness and guidance. Give me the wisdom to get my priorities right and duck the dangers of techno-devices. Help me to deliberately create periods of stillness and quietness for prayer and meditation in your presence, so that I can enjoy your presence and fellowship. May your Spirit guide me and lead me as I choose to surrender to your will every day of my life. In Jesus' precious name, I pray. Amen.

CHAPTER 6

MATERIAL DISTRACTIONS

*T*he earth is the Lord's, and the fulness thereof; the world, and they that dwell therein"** (Ps. 24:1).**

The earth is flooded with God's grace and abundantly showered with His blessings. He has not withheld His arm from bestowing every good and perfect gift upon mankind, ranging from food to clothing, shelter, authority, and possessions.

At creation, He freely granted these gifts to man, because He wanted mankind to relish His favors and give praise to His great name. Aside from these multiple blessings, He also placed certain desires for power, pleasure, and possession in the human heart. God was exceedingly joyful as He placed man over every other creature and as well commanded them to "subdue the earth."

However, when Satan, our archenemy, came to colonize the earth, he polluted these areas in our lives and strategically used God's blessings as a medium of distraction. He snatched away the dignity of authority and power by using material possessions as a way of turning our focus from God. Instead of focusing on the Giver of all good things, we began to drift towards created things as if they will last forever. Instead of marveling at the fullness of the earth created by God, we indulged in idolatry by rushing after authority and power, clinging onto material things, forgetting the brevity and futility of life on earth.

Even though it may sound unpalatable, the truth remains that power, authority, and possessions are God-given blessings. Nevertheless, Satan is cunningly using these material blessings as temptations against us. Our inbuilt motivations and desires, given to us for a greater purpose are now used by the enemy as a special tool to degenerate us to hedonism.

Literally, the word possession actually means "goods or belongings that you are in control of or something over which you have ownership." Therefore, in simpler words, when God commanded Adam to subdue the earth, He was commissioning him to take possession of everything laid before his eyes. It was God's willful decision to hand over His entire creation to man. But Satan, the father of liars and master of craftiness, subtly overturned the intent of God into an evil weapon of distraction. Rather than possessing their possessions, humankind is now being possessed by their possessions. But God's word in Obadiah 17 offers the solution to this dilemma: *"But upon mount Zion shall be deliverance, and there shall be holiness; and the house of Jacob shall possess their possessions."*

As the world progresses, jealousy and hatred are multiplying, and man's desire to gather everything to himself is exponentially increasing at the same time. Therefore, this chapter focuses on another dangerous distraction – material possession. This distraction evidently manifests itself as mankind advances in every area of life.

The chapter is aimed at awakening your spirit to the realization that "everything on earth is vanity," as the preacher cried out in the book of Ecclesiastes. Do not be deceived by the short-term pleasures of this world, but you need to realize that even though everything in the world belongs to the Lord, there are certain things that the ruler of this world is actively using to divert our focus and attention from our Rock. Therefore, be on guard and do not be distracted by satanic strategies. Additionally, we need to carefully identify diverse blessings and gifts of the Lord that Satan is using to get us distracted from God's presence, path, plan and purpose for our lives.

"And the cares of this world, and the deceitfulness of riches, and the lusts of other things entering in, choke the word, and it becometh unfruitful" (**Mark 4:19**).

Even though the earth belongs to God, the things of the world have been terribly tainted by evil. Therefore, joy cannot be found in worldly things as they are baits to lure people into sin. Most importantly, you should ask God to grant you wisdom and also help you to hold onto His eternal promises when the perishable beauty of life entices you.

The Biblical account of Jesus' temptation recorded in Matthew 4:1-11 is a perfect example that fully illustrates Satan's strategy of distraction through material possession.

It is interesting to note the audacity of Satan when he spoke to the King of kings and equally offered Him things that were created by Him in order to deny Him of the eternal glory that awaited Him in Heaven.

Satan had ample knowledge of man's nature and the tendency to be drawn to material things. He knew that Jesus was bound by human flesh and had the same instincts as a man. When he approached Jesus, first, he used the necessity of food to distract Him. Second, he created doubt in His mind regarding God's promises. Third, he aimed at man's ingrained desire for material possession.

The devil took Jesus to the pinnacle of a lofty mountain and showed Him the entire kingdoms of the world. He began to show off his authority to Him by proposing a deal that he would give Jesus all the kingdoms of the world if He could bow down to worship him.

However, Jesus was filled with the Holy Spirit; hence, He rebuked him. The Lord of heaven and earth knew that even though the earthly flesh was weak, His Spirit had the power to keep Him rooted and fixed on His calling. Jesus was here for a purpose and He did not allow Satan's schemes to divert His focus from His mission.

Moreover, throughout the whole scenario, Jesus presented a perfect way to deal with Satan's distractions, as he tempted Him with fame, power and possession. Jesus actively engaged the Word of God as a counterattack against the schemes of the devil. He did not argue or waste time contemplating on Satan's offers. Instead, He used the sword of the Spirit and this quickly made the devil flee from Him.

"And take the helmet of salvation, and the sword of the Spirit, which is the Word of God" (**Eph. 6:17**).

Similarly, when life's vain attractions and alluring beauty invite you towards itself, you should diligently look at the author and finisher of your faith.

As Jesus tackled Satan's devices with the Word of God, you must also find refuge in His irresistible word during your moments of attacks and assaults.

The Scripture in Matthew 4:1-11 is not only teaching us about Satan's schemes and the method of dealing with them, but it also reassures us of the inherent desires that make us vulnerable to temptation.

Here is an important question that we should answer: why did God implant these desires in us in the first place? Why did He design us to be so easily drawn to things that can pose a threat to our walk with Him?

The Bible contains a lot of proofs, illustrations, and examples of reasons why God made man this way. The foremost reason is His great love for humanity. He gave us free will because of His love for us. His intent was not to give an open invitation to sin, but when sin came through man's wrong choice and disobedience, Satan used those desires for his own evil schemes.

Originally, attraction towards power, pleasure, and possession was already placed in our hearts before it turned sinful (see Genesis 3:1-7). Despite this change of purpose and character, there are a number of biblical records of where Jesus still promised us possession and power, but ultimately in heaven, sin is no longer there to ruin the purity of the desire.

"And every one that hath forsaken houses, or brethren, or sister, or father, or mother, or wife, or children, or lands, for my name's sake, shall receive an hundredfold, and shall inherit everlasting life" **(Mt 19:29).**

Certainly, God intended these blessings for humans created in His image and not for the fallen man. The desire for possession was planted in us by God to motivate us to achieve our ultimate reward in heaven. Therefore, to view the desire for possession as an entirely evil tendency is absolutely unbiblical.

However, it is true that God still appeals to this desire, but He emphasizes on its importance in the afterlife when He will sift the evil from the good and there will be no single soul involved in idolatry.

"Lay not up for yourselves treasures upon earth, where moth and rust doth corrupt, and where thieves break through and steal: but lay up for yourselves treasures in heaven, where neither moth nor rust doth corrupt, and where thieves do not break through nor steal: for where your treasure is, there will your heart be also" **(Matt. 6:19-21).**

Interestingly, Jesus teaches us to look towards the eternal treasure in heaven and make it our source of motivation and hope. As the world progresses, our hopes are crumpled up, especially when we see the inevitable doom looming over the world. Then, it becomes apparent that clinging to things of the world is utter foolishness. Beloved, fix your heart on heavenly possessions because they are eternal.

"And, behold, one came and said unto him, 'Good Master, what good thing shall I do, that I may have eternal life?' And he said unto him, 'Why callest thou me good? There is none good but one, that is, God: but if thou wilt enter into life, keep the commandments. He saith unto him, which?' Jesus said, "Thou shalt do no murder; thou shalt not commit adultery; thou shalt not steal; thou shalt not bear false witness; honor thy father and

thy mother; and, thou shalt love thy neighbor as thyself.' The young man saith unto him, 'All these things have I kept from my youth up: what lack I yet?' Jesus said unto him, 'If thou wilt be perfect, go and sell that thou hast, and give to the poor, and thou shalt have treasure in heaven: and come and follow me.' But when the young man heard that saying, he went away sorrowful: for he had great possessions. Then said Jesus unto his disciples, 'Verily I say unto you, that a rich man shall hardly enter into the kingdom of heaven. And again I say unto you, It is easier for a camel to go through the eye of a needle, than for a rich man to enter into the kingdom of God'" (**Matt. 19:16-24**).

This story shows Jesus' reaction to an important issue of life. Jesus emphatically stated how difficult it is for a rich man to enter the kingdom of heaven. The rich man claimed to have followed all the commandments of God. Yet, Jesus asked him to sell all his possessions and give the money to the poor.

Obviously, Jesus knew the accompanying dangers of possessions, because if not properly handled, possession will eventually turn to possessors. Hence, Jesus emphasized the profitability of denying earthly treasures and selfish desires.

Sadly, attempts to acquire power and possession had resulted in envy, hatred, strife, and murder. The love of money is the root of all evils, and it could darken the mind of the godliest person, if not curbed. Therefore, Jesus commanded the rich young man to give up all his wealth, which had turned into his idol, if he truly desired to enter heaven.

Factually, this is one of the numerous examples of self-denial recorded in the New Testament. We are told to deny ourselves and take up our crosses if we want to follow

Christ. Denying ourselves includes giving up our desires of acquiring huge possessions, great accomplishments, global fame or billions of U.S dollars.

<u>HOLDING ON TO JESUS</u>

Realistically, we cannot trifle with riches and still think that it will not bring us into temptation. As followers and fellow cross-bearers of Christ, we ought to leave earthly vain treasures behind and store up blessings in the eternal storehouse of heaven. We are to hold on to our hope in Christ that we will surely receive our full reward when we stand before Him at His throne of Judgment.

Truly, Apostle Paul deeply understood lots of hidden dangers that always accompany the ladder of fame and recognition. He knew that the more you gain wealth and power, the more susceptible to the devil's plans you will become. Therefore, you need to prepare yourself for warfare that accompanies greatness.

"For a great door and effectual is opened unto me, and there are many adversaries" (**1 Cor. 16:9**).

This great Apostle of Christ was fully aware that his calling had exposed him to more attacks and temptations of the devil. Besides, he had insight into the fact that His talents and skills were not suitable weapons to combat the forces of darkness.

Graciously, he discovered that the Lord's grace was sufficient, and it was His Word alone that could tear down the strongholds of Satan in his life. So, as elevation comes, so do many trials, but if God is the One elevating you, then you must rest assured that He will carry you through the difficult path. Yes, as long as you have Him in your boat, you are safe and secure, regardless of the raging storm.

Oswald Chambers, an early twentieth-century Scottish Baptist and Holiness Movement evangelist and teacher, opined that: *"When you get higher up, you face other temptations and characteristics. Satan uses the strategy of elevation in temptation, and God does the same, but the effect is different. When the devil puts you into an elevated place, he makes you screw your idea of holiness beyond what flesh and blood could ever bear, it is a spiritual acrobatic performance, you are poised and dare not move; but when God elevates you by His grace into the heavenly places, instead of finding a pinnacle to cling to, you find a great tableland where it is easy to move."*

In today's age, many Christian organizations are victims of satanic snares, simply because their leaders have bowed to satanic temptations. Their desires to possess wealth have given rise to more sinful practices such as sexual immorality, human trafficking, drug peddling, abortion and a bunch of detestable sins.

Pathetically, the Internet is filled with scandalous news reports of many Christian evangelists who have traded their vocation with the temporal riches of this world. They have failed to properly handle their godly responsibilities and at the same time tarnishing the name of God.

They have hoarded money in the name of exhibiting prosperity and have consequently kindled the wrath of God. Thus, we have a lesson to learn from these people that, no matter how much good we try to do, wealth can persuade and entrap us to do things that are against God's will. The strategy of the evil one is deceit and guile; once we are within his field of attack and are unguarded by God's Word, we can easily be led into temptations.

"Thy testimonies also are my delight and my counselors" (**Ps. 119:24**).

Therefore, like King David, always seek counsel from God. Also, allow Christ to reign in your heart, and beware of covetousness. God is the giver of all good things. Jesus was emphatic about this truth; hence, He boldly stated that no one can receive anything except it is given to him from above. He added that no one can bear any fruit without Him. We are mere branches; He is the vine that is giving us nutrients and vitality. Be informed, all of us are privileged receivers of divine blessings.

Apparently, since the earth and its fullness belong to God, we can only possess anything through inheritance, and this is only possible when we become a member of God's family. Anyone who tries to acquire something through other means will automatically become possessed by that thing; it could be money, houses, lands, automobiles, etc. This simply implies that they are not acquiring God's blessings, but actually paving a way for themselves. This will inevitably lead them to hell.

<u>WATCH YOUR HEART</u>

"Whatsoever things are true, whatsoever things are honest, whatsoever things are just, whatsoever things are pure, whatsoever things are lovely, whatsoever things are of good report; if there be any virtue, and if there be any praise, think on these things" (**Phil. 4:8**).

The Word of God admonishes us to think about whatever is "true." Vine's Complete Expository Dictionary explains that we are to "make those (true) things the subjects of our thoughtful consideration" or "carefully reflect on them."

Unfailingly, it is through reflection and constant meditation that we can guard our hearts and minds against sinful desires. We are human, and it is our nature to be drawn towards possessions, but once the Spirit of God awakens us to the reality of life, we are no longer attracted to worldly riches, but our hopes are fixed on the eternal kingdom. As you train your mind according to the Word of God, you should also allow Christ to dwell in your heart so that there is hardly any room for any sort of distraction.

Therefore, it is certain that the only refuge of humanity is the Word of God.

"But upon mount Zion shall be deliverance, and there shall be holiness; and the house of Jacob shall possess their possessions" **(Obad. 17).**

This is God's recipe for freedom from bondage and acquiring earthly possessions.

"For this cause I bow my knees unto the Father of our Lord Jesus Christ, of whom the whole family in heaven and earth is named, that he would grant you, according to the riches of his glory, to be strengthened with might by his Spirit in the inner man; that Christ may dwell in your hearts by faith; that ye, being rooted and grounded in love, may be able to comprehend with all saints what is the breadth, and length, and depth, and height; and to know the love of Christ, which passeth knowledge, that ye might be filled with all the fulness of God" **(Eph. 3:14-19).**

Summarily, let the fullness of Christ flood your heart, so that you will be able to act like Him. Jesus is God and man, with the same fleshly inclinations and tendencies, yet He chose to cling to the eternal hope.

Similarly, you must totally surrender to the Spirit of God as He leads you through the wilderness, temptations, sufferings, and death into eternal life that we have received through Jesus Christ.

CHAPTER 7

THE TWO-EDGED SWORD

Amidst the demonic powers of this dark world, the Word of God stands as a lighthouse emitting its radiance to light our path. It shines forth with full vigor when the evil forces come to attack us, and it is the only refuge and hope that focuses our gaze towards Jesus when there are numerous distractions encompassing us. It guides us by revealing the will of God to us. Moreover, it corrects us like a teacher and as well protects us like a shield when we declare it boldly.

God's Word is extremely powerful, and it is able to overthrow kingdoms and can also turn around the course of events in a twinkling of an eye. Professing it loudly and proclaiming it with authority is what unleashes the power and makes us conquerors over everything that tries to exalt itself against the knowledge of God in our lives.

It is our offensive weapon to fight the devil's schemes; hence, it is imperative we learn to use it more effectively.

Previously, we have studied the operations of Satan's guile via distraction and its various modes of manipulation. Now, it is important for us to study the significance of God's Word – the two-edged sword.

Interestingly, the Bible lists various ways the Word of God could be defined and how it is imperative for us. Furthermore, the most prominent way of using this term in the Bible is as a personal title for the Lord Jesus Christ – the Word. This is an important fundamental concept that must be grasped in order to thoroughly comprehend the importance of God's Word in your life as a believer.

"And the Word was made flesh, and dwelt among us, (and we beheld his glory, the glory as of the only begotten of the Father), full of grace and truth" **(Jn. 1:14).**

Here, the Bible describes Him as the incarnated Word of God, who was made to fulfill the great plan of salvation. Therefore, when we hold the Bible in our hands, this truth suddenly exposes our minds to the power and truthfulness of God's Word. It is not a book with dead letters that try to convince us but fails to influence us.

In fact, the Bible is the living Word, active, new and ever-renewing. It is fresh manna from heaven that sustains our spiritual health. It corrects, exhorts, and sets us free. Moreover, while the enemy uses myriads of evil strategies and demonic schemes against us, the Word of God constantly shields us and makes us invincible.

THE MECHANISM OF GOD'S WORD

"For the Word of God is quick, and powerful, and sharper than any two-edged sword, piercing even to the dividing asunder of soul and spirit, and of the joints and marrow, and is a discerner of the thoughts and intents of the heart" **(Heb. 4:12).**

The above description of the Word of God is a complete insight into how it functions. It describes the power and authority of God's Word in a way that may cause fear in the hearts of people. Some spiritual infants may wonder why the word that is supposed to be a source of comfort and strength is working as a sword piercing through the soul. It is not supposed to be painful to the heart, but hopeful and comforting.

However, this verse is only emphasizing the power of God's Word. It is not just to comfort us, but to equally transform us. The Word of God is not meant to be simply read out or recited, but as we speak it, the real word permeates our minds and actively begins to transform us from inside to outside. It goes deeper into the soul and spirit, piercing through the joints and marrow, and working its way into the thoughts and intentions of our hearts.

But why does the Bible use various biological terms to describe God's Word? Actually, to some, this may be viewed or interpreted in terms of how vast and powerful the reach of the word of God is. But this verse is not meant to teach us this fact superficially. It must be examined and meditated upon to truly understand the mighty power embedded in the Word.

The first function that the verse teaches us is the range of penetration. Apostle Paul compares the Word of God to a double-edged sword that pierces even to the dividing asunder of soul and spirit, joints and marrow, and is a discerner of the thoughts and intents of the heart. Nothing is hidden, impenetrable or untouchable when exposed to God's Word. It has the ability to penetrate deeply in order to assess and examine what lies in the inner chambers of our being.

Generally, it analyzes the innermost parts of our being and often discerns what lies inside of us, whether good or bad. It can spot unbelief, hypocrisy, and unfaithfulness.

The word "discern" means to make a judgment and this is exactly what the Word of God does. It does not condemn or make us feel guilty like the vices of the evil one. Instead, when it meets the darkest parts of us, it purifies, sanctifies, corrects and transforms it.

Predictably, the devil wants us to have an unbelieving heart; this is the basis of his incessant attacks through distractions such as anxiety, fear, technology, and worldliness. Satan's deceitfulness can harden our hearts, but the word of God breaks the hardened part of us that exalts itself against the will of God.

On this note, The Book of Hebrews rightly advised us about the imminent dangers of unbelief and how frequent intake and exposure to God's word can circumcise our hearts.

"Take heed, brethren, lest there be in any of you an evil heart of unbelief, in departing from the living God. But exhort one another daily, while it is called today; lest any of you be hardened through the deceitfulness of sin" **(Heb. 3:12-13).**

The Word of God has the power to separate the bad from the good, just as the chaff is usually removed from grains. It takes off the mask of hypocrisy and self-righteousness and unravels the reality of sin. So, whether there is sexual immorality, cheating, dishonesty, or vengeance, the Word of God can bring them to the surface and purge them, despite our inability to recognize them as sin.

THE WORD IS LIGHT

The illumination power of God's Word to expose and as well purge sin is one of the reasons why many people are not willing to read the Scriptures. They can spend a few minutes in daily prayer, but when it comes to reading the Bible, they will never muster the strength to open it on their own.

The Word of God will always convict sinners. It is disheartening that when it reveals the sinful areas of believers, they are always stiff-necked. They can listen to sugar-coated, feel-good sermons for hours, but the one message that taps at their conscience is ignored at all costs. Sincerely, this generation needs striking and heart pricking messages more than they think.

"For every one that doeth evil hateth the light, neither cometh to the light, lest his deeds should be reproved" **(Jn. 3:20).**

The Word of God is a perfect light that exposes our deeds. It fills us with conviction and softens our hardened hearts.

Peter's Pentecostal sermon is a typical example of the transforming effect of God's holy Word on people.

"Now when they heard this, they were pricked in their heart, and said unto Peter and to the rest of the apostles, Men and brethren, what shall we do?" **(Acts. 2:37).**

Amazingly, the mammoth crowd that heard the gospel message was compelled to think and re-think about what they must do and keep doing with their lives. Their slumbering souls were awakened as the word entered their ears. However, it must be kept in mind that unlike the guilt-inducing lies of the enemy, the Word of God only aims at transforming us.

Additionally, it is for our discipline and reproof; this is why it must be the foundation of our lives. It has the potency of bringing our sinfulness to our awareness and when this happens, it leads us to the point of repentance. The Word of God may meet us in whatever state we are, but if appropriately received, it never leaves us in the same state. Every passing day, it makes us conform to the perfect image of Jesus.

Although the Bible has been a complete guide filled with reproofs, instructions, inspirations, and commandments, believers are yet to fully enjoy its transforming power. Again, Apostle Paul spoke in a relatively stern manner when he addressed the church. These are vital lessons for believers of different ages to learn and adapt.

"Thou therefore which teachest another, teachest thou not thyself? Thou that preachest a man should not steal, dost thou steal? Thou that sayest a man should not commit adultery, dost thou commit adultery? Thou that abhorrest idols, dost thou commit sacrilege?" **(Rom. 2:21-22).**

The authority of the Word of God is one of its unequaled characteristics. Unlike other books and secular words of advice, the Word of God instructs, disciplines, and corrects us in order to prevent us from falling into temptation and as well help us differentiate the voice of God from that of the devil. The Word of God makes us wiser, both in our physical dealings with people and our spiritual relationship with God.

OBEY THE WORD

"All Scripture is given by inspiration of God, and is profitable for doctrine, for reproof, for correction, for instruction in righteousness, that the man of God may be perfect, thoroughly furnished unto all good works" **(2 Tim. 3:16-17).**

If you painstakingly observe this portion of the Scripture, you will clearly see what the Word of God is meant to do in your life. It is given to "equip you thoroughly for every good work." The work has not been finished when the Word was imparted to us but listening and teaching constitute the first stage. In fact, when the Word of God is planted like a seed in the heart of believers, it gradually buds, blossoms, and bears fruits, bringing forth like a beautiful fruit-bearing plant and these fruits are the fruits of the Spirit. Graciously, we grow and mature in accordance with the Lord's commandments.

"But be ye doers of the word, and not hearers only, deceiving your own selves" (**Jms. 1:22**).

Although hearing is the first process of faith production, oftentimes, the devil cunningly snatches away the word that was originally meant for a greater purpose. Unknown to us, even before we reap the dividends of the word we heard or let it change our hearts, the devil may try to pollute it through lies and consequently distract us from focusing on it.

Thus, it is essential to implement the Word of God, once you read or listen to it. Fortunately, when you make the Word of God an active part of your life and understand the power it holds, you will live victoriously and become fulfilled in life.

SOME HIDDEN IMPORTANCE OF GOD'S WORD

There are several other reasons why the Word of God is important for people of all ages. A popular belief is that the Bible must not be given to little children because they are too young to decipher most of the great mysteries and unchangeable commandments embedded in it by God.

Due to this erroneous belief, parents often introduce the Bible to their children once they reach an assumed age of accountability. However, what parents need to understand is that the word of God is equally given to children and younger people.

"But continue thou in the things which thou hast learned and hast been assured of, knowing of whom thou hast learned them; and that from a child thou hast known the holy Scriptures, which are able to make thee wise unto salvation through faith which is in Christ Jesus" (**2 Tim. 3:14-15**).

Painfully, we are living in a perilous age where children's cartoons are greatly influenced or polluted by evil. There is no doubt that you might have watched cartoons or movies that contain elements that are only appropriate for adults. Rapidly, they proliferate and these innocent children are subconsciously fed with sinful information.

It is imperative to know that the devil is so crafty. Without delay, he begins his work from the early days of human lives. Therefore, why must we prevent our children from knowing the Lord and growing in the wisdom and knowledge of His Word?

Specifically, the Lord directed youngsters to dig into His Word for conscious obedience and faithfulness.

"Wherewithal shall a young man cleanse his way? By taking heed thereto according to thy word" (**Ps. 119:9**).

Nowadays, younger people are more vulnerable to satanic colonization and influence. Particularly in Western schools and colleges, Satan is cleverly poisoning their minds and making them become rebellious and disobedient.

Usually, you will find so many young girls and boys involved in sinful practices, but you will hardly find a godly child.

Despite their vulnerability, it is often said about nations that, "The biggest asset of the church and of a nation is her young generation." They are the middle ground and the future of a nation. Nonetheless, Satan is cleverly laying his hold on this asset and calmly luring them into assorted sins, so that godliness will soon become a forgotten virtue on the face of the earth.

Certainly, Satan is intensely attacking this group of people so that the whole world might be adversely affected. Thus, we need to teach and lavish God's Word on our children as the veritable weapon to overthrow the kingdom of Satan on earth and to thwart his plan and purpose against us.

Compulsorily, we must teach and discipline our children so that as they grow up, they will remain in God's light and keep walking in accordance with His will.

"Train up a child in the way he should go: and when he is old, he will not depart from it" (**Prov. 22:6**).

JESUS: OUR HIGH PRIEST

Yes, we have a High Priest who knows, understands and had experienced every temptation that could be presented to man. Despite being God, He did not rely on any other way to extricate Himself from the trap of the devil. Instead, He used the sword of the Spirit: the Word of God. Therefore, we ought to do likewise, not relying on our own strength and wisdom, but depending on the power of the Word. Be reminded, Jesus Christ is our perfect example.

"And he humbled thee, and suffered thee to hunger, and fed thee with manna, which thou knewest not, neither did thy fathers know, that he might make thee know that man doth not live by bread only, but by every word that proceedeth out of the mouth of the Lord doth man live" **(Deut. 8:3).**

This is one of the Bible verses that Jesus engaged when Satan tried to lure Him into sin. Jesus compared the Word of God to the heavenly bread that was given to the Israelites while traveling to the Promised Land. The Word of God is a necessity for our souls. If you glance at the current state of the world, people's bellies may be filled with dainties, but their souls are starving.

Additionally, they are far from the Word of God and are preoccupied with the worries and cares of this world. They seek for peace in vain and joy in worldly things. It is similar to a man who has a chronic disease but still eats the food that aggravates his condition. Evidently, his journey to health starts with self-discipline. What he requires is proper diet and medication to be healed.

Therefore, finding fulfillment in earthly things is a useless pursuit. The power of God's Word urgently and desperately needs to be recognized in order to curb the plague of sin that has corrupted the totality of mankind at creation.

BE WATCHFUL

In contemporary times, Satan is not only using political tactics or secular manipulations to alter the beliefs of people but is actively using the Word of God to lead people astray through the agency of false teachers. Just as he tempted Jesus by camouflaging and misinterpreting the Word of God, he is aggressively using the Word of God to cause division within the church. This deception gives rise to many denominations and sects. Each person takes what suits him/her and uses it for his/her personal benefits.

Besides, the Devil has also used other religions to spread extremism and force people to abandon their faith. Satan is attacking the Judeo-Christian foundations around the world. In the name of tolerance, the enemy is diluting the entire populations of European countries with radical Islamists. He is relentlessly propagating doctrines that are contrary to noble ideologies upon which those nations are built.

Predictably, in a matter of time, those nations will be forcefully converted to Islam. The Islamists are using politicians, media houses, entertainment industries, academia, and some so-called charity organizations to Islamize the West.

Turkey is a glaring example. America also needs to beware of Islamic elements in influential places working from inside and outside to overrun the country. Christians living in such places need to watch and pray. They need to critically examine the ideology of political parties and the theology of churches in the light of God's Word before embracing them.

HERALD THE WORD

While Satan continuously spurs his armies to rise against us, we need to recognize that our fight is against the forces in spiritual realms. All we need to do is to unsheathe the sword of the Spirit (Word of God) and assail the ravaging evils in the world. Even though the enemy has dug its claws on the face of the earth, we could be the light bearers of the good news.

"How beautiful upon the mountains are the feet of him that bringeth good tidings, that publisheth peace, that bringeth good tidings of good, that publisheth salvation, that saith unto Zion, thy God reigneth!" **(Is. 52:7).**

Rather than allowing ourselves to be politically or ideologically manipulated, we should let our faith be grounded in God's Word. We need to heed its instructions and follow the path set by Jesus, for He is the perfect role model sent by God to us.

Undoubtedly, by doing so, we will live a peaceful life without Satan's interjection. We need to seek God's guidance from His Word in every matter of life, whether it is a political affiliation, choice of spouse or job, etc. There is an irreplaceable need to use the written Word of God as our guidebook and roadmap to guide us through all life's situations and challenges.

THE WORD AND POLITICS

Naturally, as a faithful follower of God, you must analyze political ideology and religious theology with the Word of God and subsequently allow the Spirit of God to lead you according to His will.

Truly, you don't have to be politically correct or socially conform to the standards of the world. Instead, you need to be biblically correct, and equally, discipline your heart in such a way that your thoughts are consciously or subconsciously driven by the light of God's Word. As someone has said "Don't compromise in order to be recognized."

SATAN: AN ERSTWHILE CUSTODIAN OF GOD'S WORD

You may be surprised that the enemy is more versed in Scriptures than any human being, including the spiritual leaders. The reason is not farfetched; it is simply because he was an angel before God banished him from His glorious presence. He knows where the foundation lies, and that is exactly where he aims his attacks.

"If the foundations be destroyed, what can the righteous do?" **(Ps. 11:3).**

Nevertheless, we have hope through the power of God's Word. If we make the Word of God our foundation, we shall be unshakable. Therefore, whenever the devil tries to attack us, we will be immovable as our power will be drawn from the invincible Word of God.

"The grass withereth, the flower fadeth: but the word of our God shall stand for ever" **(Is. 40:8).**

CHAPTER 8

SPIRITUAL VISION

When God created man, He gave him a beautiful and wonderful form with perfectly aligned bones, joints and organs, which are rightly placed within him. In His manifold wisdom, God designed an intricate piece of art and meticulously crafted the innermost parts of his being with utmost intelligence, precision and accuracy. He gave him the ability to see, hear, smell, speak and walk as well as experience His presence.

Having bestowed him with the blessing of physical vision, He enabled him to see the beautiful work of His hand and praise Him for His marvelous deeds.

THE SPIRITUAL DIMENSION OF CREATION

The process of creation was not just physical, as our minds would have us believe. There was also a spiritual component, which brought us life. That was the breath of the Almighty God.

At creation, God breathed into the nostrils of man, thereby, giving him His own life and Spirit. He created man to operate beyond the limitations of the three-dimensional world that is visible to our eyes. He gave us another dimension, an "invisible" state, which is far more glorious than the physical state.

This realm is real, vibrant and more powerful than anything we can perceive with our physical eyes, even with 20/20 vision.

THE SUPERIORITY OF THE SPIRITUAL REALM

The spiritual realm isn't temporal; it will definitely outlive our physical bodies. However, the spiritual realm can only be accessed and enjoyed by those who live and walk in the spirit. Science has convinced the minds of the natural man to believe that we are only flesh and bones and that once we die, we become food for worms and manure to fertilize the plants.

This naïve conclusion spurs hopelessness and it is also a dangerous sign of unbelief in God's abilities. It also narrows our perception and scope of vision and is a contradiction to God's Word.

"For we wrestle not against flesh and blood, but against principalities, against powers, against the rulers of the darkness of this world, against spiritual wickedness in high places" (**Eph. 6:12**).

Emphatically, the Bible talks about the existence and operation of the spiritual realm and declares that it is more important than the physical realm. In unambiguous term, the Holy Bible reveals that all battles, struggles and challenges that are confronting us in the physical world are in reality a fight against the evil forces in the spiritual realm.

MATERIAL PROSPERITY: THE UNIVERSAL BAIT

When it comes to receiving blessings, we must fix our eyes on the spiritual realm, because all that we see in the present world is merely shadows of the real blessings that God has in store for us.

"If therefore ye have not been faithful in the unrighteous mammon, who will commit to your trust the true riches?" (**Lk. 16:11**).

The verse above is communicating a deeper truth about prosperity. From God's perspective, abundant prosperity is not a product of hustling, hard work or human labor. It is purely a spiritual transaction; this kind of prosperity is given to believers who have been faithful in handling the unrighteous mammon – money.

Satan's strategy to lead us astray and divert our focus from true riches in the heavenly realms is real. He has a devilish plan to actively keep us busy with unending activities of life in order to switch our focus from living a life that glorifies God.

FAITH: THE WINNING WEAPON OF BELIEVERS

Interestingly, understanding the strategies of the enemy and how to ward off his darts are not sufficient ingredients for a victorious Christian life. Compulsorily, we must study and understand the concept, importance and operation of faith, because every other weapon of our warfare is dependent on faith.

In our quest to live successful and victorious Christian lives, we must arm ourselves with the understanding of the significance of the spiritual realm and the spiritual vision of Faith.

Our bodies are surely blessed with two eyes that enable us to see the world around us, but there is a spiritual vision that the Bible teaches and encourages us to experience. Provided we want to survive the evil and wickedness of this world, we must possess the seeing eyes: spiritual vision.

Beyond debate, it is evident that your salvation is solely based upon your faith in Christ's death and resurrection. Failure to believe this equates your good deeds to absolute nonsense.

"But without faith it is impossible to please Him: for he that cometh to God must believe that He is, and that He is a rewarder of them that diligently seek him" **(Heb. 11-6).**

UNDERSTANDING FAITH

It is amazing how we fail to realize that life is all about faith. For instance, you cannot sit on your office chair, if you don't have faith that it has enough strength to carry your weight. If you don't have faith in the competence of the pilot, or the soundness of the engine of the aircraft, you will not even sit relaxed in the plane.

Moreover, when it comes to meaningful relationships, it is imperative to have certain degrees of faith in people. Having faith in people doesn't mean you have everything sorted out about them, but your faith drives you on in the relationship.

Webster Dictionary defines faith as belief and trust in and loyalty to God, belief in the traditional doctrines of religion or a firm belief in something for which there is no proof.

Basically, faith implies believing in what you cannot see or know. It is through the spiritual vision that we believe that we have already received all that we ask for in the spiritual realms.

"Now faith is the substance of things hoped for, the evidence of things not seen" **(Heb. 11:1).**

The Bible also teaches that faith in God comes by hearing His Word. The more we meditate on the word of God, the stronger our faith will become.

"So then faith cometh by hearing, and hearing by the word of God" **(Rom. 10:17).**

HOW TO MAXIMIZE THE POWER OF FAITH

Therefore, once you have realized the importance of the power of the Word of God, you must also understand that the power of God can only be unleashed in you, if you have faith in His promises. You have to believe that all your true blessings are resident in Jesus and these blessings are everlasting in nature. All physical things are temporary, while, spiritual things, though unseen, are eternal. This concept of spiritual vision may be a little baffling to non-believers because they are spiritually discerned.

"But the natural man receiveth not the things of the Spirit of God: for they are foolishness unto him: neither can he know them, because they are spiritually discerned" **(1 Cor. 2:14).**

SUPERNATURAL VISION

Walking in Christ helps us discern spiritual things. Therefore, we are able to overcome the attacks of the devil, if we can promptly detect them. In the physical world, "seeing is believing" is a common saying and this physical truth can be applied in the spiritual realm as well.

However, our lenses of vision in both realms are different from each other. To see in the physical, you need physical lenses, but to see in the spiritual you need spiritual lenses.

Throughout the gospel, there were various accounts of people who did not understand Jesus and His teachings, despite several signs and wonders He performed in their midst. One example is His encounter with Nicodemus as recorded in John 3:1-12:

"There was a man of the Pharisees, named Nicodemus, a ruler of the Jews: the same came to Jesus by night, and said unto Him, 'Rabbi, we know that thou art a teacher come from God: for no man can do these miracles that thou doest, except God be with him.' Jesus answered and said unto him, 'Verily, verily, I say unto thee, except a man be born again, he cannot see the kingdom of God.' Nicodemus saith unto him, 'How can a man be born when he is old? Can he enter the second time into his mother's womb, and be born?' Jesus answered, 'Verily, verily, I say unto thee, except a man be born of water and of the Spirit, he cannot enter into the kingdom of God. That which is born of the flesh is flesh; and that which is born of the Spirit is spirit. Marvel not that I said unto thee, ye must be born again. The wind bloweth where it listeth, and thou hearest the sound thereof, but canst not tell whence it cometh, and whither it goeth: so is every one that is born of the Spirit.' Nicodemus answered

and said unto him, 'How can these things be?' Jesus answered and said unto him, 'Art thou a master of Israel, and knowest not these things? Verily, verily, I say unto thee, we speak that we do know, and testify that we have seen; and ye receive not our witness. If I have told you earthly things, and ye believe not, how shall ye believe, if I tell you of heavenly things?'"

Nicodemus couldn't comprehend the message of Jesus because of his darkened mind and spiritual blindness. Similarly, the scribes and Pharisees exhibited ignorance to every teaching of Jesus, consequently, they hated Him. They could not recognize Him as the true Messiah foretold by various prophets.

Therefore, we must examine ourselves to know whether our eyes are open or blind to the truth of God's Word. If we find out that we are blind to the truth of God's Word, we need to confess our sins and ask Jesus to forgive us and open our spiritual eyes.

"If we confess our sins, He is faithful and just to forgive us our sins, and to cleanse us from all unrighteousness" **(1 Jn. 1:9).**

Once this happens, we shall receive the gift of the Holy Spirit and be granted the grace to see beyond the physical realm: spiritual vision. Subsequently, we can perceive the things of the Kingdom of God and walk more closely with Him.

1 Corinthians 2:14 says: *"But the natural man receiveth not the things of the Spirit of God: for they are foolishness unto him: neither can he know them, because they are spiritually discerned."*

An eagle is a classic example of an animal that possesses super vision. Only an eagle can see a rabbit from about two miles away, which is not possible for human eyes to spot. This is made possible because of its excellent vision. Similarly, a person with an excellent spiritual vision will be able to see spiritual things which carnal eyes cannot see.

<u>SPIRITUAL VISION ENHANCES SPIRITUAL FOCUS</u>

Amazingly, once you can see into the heavenly realm via spiritual vision, you will realize the utter worthlessness of a life solely devoted to the pursuit of material possessions. You will see beyond temporal things of this fleeting age into the priceless treasures reserved for us in heaven.

Therefore, you will remain unperturbed, no matter how hard the challenges of life could be. Sometimes, everything around you may look knotty and disturbing, that you find yourself trapped in anxiety and depression, but with your spiritual vision, you will stay positive and hopeful, knowing that you are a victor and not a victim, and bask in the confidence of the reality that you are more than a conqueror in Christ Jesus.

"For our light affliction, which is but for a moment, worketh for us a far more exceeding and eternal weight of glory; while we look not at the things which are seen, but at the things which are not seen. For the things which are seen are temporal; but the things which are not seen are eternal **(2 Cor. 4:17-18).**

There is a plethora of biblical examples, of people whose spiritual vision empowered them to fulfill God's great plan for their lives. Patriarchs like Abraham, Isaac, Jacob, Moses, Joseph, David, Paul and others had faith in God's promises even when their circumstances appeared to literally negate

God's plan and offered no inkling of hope. Yet they stood firm and waited patiently until God proved His absolute faithfulness to them.

"By faith Moses, when he was born, was hid three months of his parents, because they saw he was a proper child; and they were not afraid of the king's commandment. By faith Moses, when he was come to years, refused to be called the son of Pharaoh's daughter, choosing rather to suffer affliction with the people of God, than to enjoy the pleasures of sin for a season, esteeming the reproach of Christ greater riches than the treasures in Egypt, for he had respect unto the recompense of the reward. By faith he forsook Egypt, not fearing the wrath of the king, for he endured, as seeing him who is invisible. Through faith he kept the Passover, and the sprinkling of blood, lest he that destroyed the firstborn should touch them. By faith they passed through the Red sea as by dry land, which the Egyptians assaying to do were drowned" **(Heb. 11:23-29).**

These verses explicitly show how Moses acted by faith. Be reminded, without faith, it is impossible to please God. Faith is and will remain the access code to and relating with God.

Once upon a time, the nation of Israel was surrounded by the armies of the king of Syria and Elisha's servant was greatly terrified, but the Prophet remained calm. Elisha then prayed that God should open the eyes of his servant so that he could know and see the superiority of the hosts of God. Expectedly, God honored Prophet Elisha's prayer by opening the eyes of his servant. Graciously, when his spiritual vision was activated, he saw God's invisible armies. Consequently, he became calm, confident and unperturbed.

"And Elisha prayed, and said, 'Lord, I pray thee, open his eyes, that he may see.' And the Lord opened the eyes of the young man, and he saw, and behold, the mountain was full of horses and chariots of fire round about Elisha" **(2 Kings 6:17).**

This verse glaringly shows the difference between natural and spiritual vision. Carefully observe that Elisha's servant and the king of Israel thought that the large army of Syria would overrun them, because they could not see into the spiritual realm. But when Elisha prayed, God opened the eyes of the young man and he saw countless horses and chariots; thereafter, he believed that they were safe in God's hands.

This story should instill confidence in and motivate every Christian that with God on our side, we are more than conquerors, no matter how fierce the battle may be.

Our focus determines our destiny. It determines whether we live a life of victory or defeat. If we focus on the boisterous storm, we will sink, but if the object of our focus is the resurrected Christ, our Red Sea would part, the walls of Jericho would fall, our Goliath will be vanquished, the roaring lions won't hurt us, and the fiery furnace won't burn us. Our faith is directly proportional to our focus.

Instead of focusing on the problems of our lives, let us shift our focus to the solution and Savior of the entire human race: Jesus Christ. He is our omnipotent King and has the ability to solve all our problems: whether sickness, sorrow, depression, spiritual or any kind of physical attacks the enemy may hurl at us.

"Now unto Him that is able to do exceeding abundantly above all that we ask or think, according to the power that worketh in us" **(Eph 3:20).**

As long as we focus on Jesus, the author and finisher of our faith, all challenges of life would become insignificant and fade into nothingness before His omnipotence.

CHAPTER 9

OUR ULTIMATE PURPOSE AND FOCUS

Focus is the ultimate nemesis of distraction. The former contradicts the latter like two parallel roads that never meet at any point. There is a great similitude between bringing distraction and focus together with traveling with one's feet in two boats. That is simply impossible, isn't it?

However, if you presumptuously attempt this, you are going to plunge into the water, as the two feet will eventually diverge. Similarly, that is what happens with distraction and focus moving together. We would either give in to the things that distract us or remain focused on our purpose.

Basically, in the presence of distraction, focus cannot be maintained. On this note, loss of focus can prevent us from reaching our Promised Land. Loss of focus may seem to be a trivial factor in our daily lives, but it plays a significant role in our daily walk with God.

Can you imagine how safe our roads would be if we can drive without distraction? As a matter of fact, we have all experienced the outcome of consistent focus and equally enjoyed the benefits of it. Focus in every aspect of life, whether in doing a house chore, writing an examination or pursuing longterm goals, can yield astounding results if continued unabated.

Therefore, it is not a surprise that the devil often attempts to shift our focus from eternal things to ephemeral things. He carefully targets our weakest moment and hurls several distractions at us, so that we cannot keep our gaze fixed on God. He wants us to be caught up by distractions around us so that our attention could be constantly diverted.

Satan knows that once we gain focus, we will gain control over ourselves and circumstances, because we will learn to appropriately say no to inhibitors that stop us from achieving our goals. We will become immovable and will advance with confidence towards the high prize.

THE ULTIMATE GOAL

As believers, there is only one Person we must cherish and give our undivided attention to, and that is our Lord Jesus Christ. The entire Bible is a living evidence of this truth and it was premised on how everything points towards this one Person, our Lord and Savior Jesus Christ, who will return to fully restore us back to God, despite the multitudinous strategies of Satan to make us fall, by losing our focus.

This gives an alarming reminder that there is absolutely nothing on earth that is worth our precious soul. Without the help of God, the best effort of man and his good works cannot radiate sufficient light in this dark and gloomy world. Only Jesus, the light of the world can sufficiently illuminate our world. Jesus, the only Son of God stands as a guiding light in the dark tunnel of life, walking ahead to lead us to eternity in heaven. There is no other way or route that can be taken to achieve this great goal of believers; hence, He must be our focal point.

At all times, we must look up to Him, having realized that we are in a perilous time. There are sins, griefs and chaos everywhere, but with Him, there is blessing, peace and hope.

Obviously, staying focused on Christ is like sending an invitation to challenges, because so many distractions will attack us in return. Focusing on Jesus may seem so easy, but maintaining the focus is the hardest thing to do. But unless we are focused, the outcome of our endeavors will be catastrophic.

According to reports, on the average, there is one interruption in our lives in every seven to eight minutes. Assuming we work for eight hours every day, there are about 60 interruptions. So, if it takes about 15 minutes to regain concentration after being distracted, it implies, we are not focused as expected, and this can lead to unfinished tasks and as well impact our lives in some negative ways.

Therefore, it is vital to think about the fact that if it is so hard to focus on our daily tasks, then how much harder will it be to be focused on the invisible Jesus? Satan detests our fellowship and intimacy with Jesus, because he knows that Jesus is the way, the truth, and the life. He wants us to be pre-occupied with other things to the extent that Jesus will become the least object of focus on our priority list.

It is very painful that Satan is riding on the wings of the existing distractions, because he is enlarging the scope of his activities as time passes by. We have already learned how we could be distracted internally; that is in the form of anxiety and fear so that we are emotionally, mentally, and spiritually crippled.

More so, we have studied about external distractions that explained how the enemy lures us to sin through possession, technology and other new-age philosophies. Amidst all of these, we learned that the only way we can overcome these distractions is by focusing our attention on Jesus, and this is what our Christian walk and faith are all about. It is when we realize His indispensability that we would endeavor to fix our gaze on Him at all times and under all circumstances. Hence, He becomes preeminent in all things, and everything else naturally becomes insignificant in our sight. It is like zooming the lens of a camera; as the object on focus is becoming clearer, the surroundings become blurred. This is what our focus on our Lord Jesus Christ should accomplish in our lives, and if otherwise, we have missed the focal point.

UNDERSTANDING FOCUS

Webster dictionary defines "focus" as: "a center of activity, attraction, or attention" or "a point of concentration." It is a word that has been frequently used since our childhood, from school to workplace. It can also be referred to as setting your mind on something.

THE SPIRITUAL SIGNIFICANCE OF FOCUS

"Set your affection on things above, not on things on the earth" **(Col. 3:2).**

This enables us to realize the futility of life, and how setting our hearts and minds on things on this earth is meaningless, because they are not going to last forever. We have an eternal treasure that is not going to perish and to which we must accord topmost priority.

Earlier than this period, Jesus commanded people not to place priority on earthly possession. He told them the danger and risk that are tied to such an act. *"Lay not up for yourselves treasures upon earth, where moth and rust doth corrupt, and where thieves break through and steal, but lay up for yourselves treasures in heaven, where neither moth nor rust doth corrupt, and where thieves do not break through nor steal; for where your treasure is, there will your heart be also"* (**Matt. 6:19-21**).

Subsequently, Jesus taught people about the need to set their minds on heavenly things. In a puzzling manner, He told them the importance of focus. A good light is a concentrated light or converging light. Any diverging light is not the best light for several reasons. In the same way, scattered light is not fit for spiritual attainment. Christianity is built on unity and focus. Your light must agree with other lights in the Christian circle.

"The light of the body is the eye: if therefore thine eye be single, thy whole body shall be full of light. But if thine eye be evil, thy whole body shall be full of darkness. If therefore the light that is in thee be darkness, how great is that darkness!" (**Matt. 6:22-23**).

Now, as we all know, the eye is the part of the body that is employed whenever we want to focus. The Bible refers to it as the "Lamp of the body," because blindness could be debilitating. It could make you totally dependent on others and as well prevent you from enjoying the beauty of life. Therefore, our eyes are the engines that operate our entire body, because they give us direction. If our eyes are distracted or enticed towards sin, then our entire being would give in to satanic deception and shift our focus away from God. Thus, if we want to maintain our focus on Jesus, we must constantly meditate on God's Word.

"Thy word have I hid in mine heart, that I might not sin against thee" (**Ps.119:11**).

But if we fail to keep God's Word in our hearts, we can easily lose our focus on God and consequently end up in sin.

BREAKING SATANIC STRONGHOLDS

One of the mostly used tactics of Satan against Christians is building strongholds in their lives. No aspect of spiritual warfare is more important than learning how to promptly recognize and destroy satanic strongholds. Failure to do so may lead to frustration, retardation of spiritual growth and overall spiritual defeat.

Satan's main objective is to deceive us and cause us to become so blind that we cannot see that those strongholds are there or become so discouraged while trying to overcome them. This may force us to succumb to them, thereby falling away from God. Thereafter, we would begin to think, "It's no use. I'm just a failure at being a Christian!"

Satan has clever plans that are only aimed at diverting our focus from the Lord Jesus Christ, because he knows the magnitude of the power that any believer can possess once the person's focus is fixed on Jesus. He knows the wonders and transformations that could take place once a believer realizes the available power via focus on the Lord Jesus. This available power can do tremendous things, including demolition of all satanic strongholds.

"For though we walk in the flesh we do not war after the flesh, for the weapons of our warfare are not carnal, but mighty through God to the pulling down of strongholds, casting down imaginations, and every high thing that exalts itself against the knowledge of God, and bringing into captivity every thought to the obedience of Christ" **(2 Cor. 10:3-5).**

THE FOCUS OF PETER

One particular incident established the importance of focus and that is the miraculous walk of Peter on the sea. Focus on Jesus will enable men and women to do what only God can do.

Here, only Jesus, the Son of God walked on the sea and focus on Him enabled Peter to do likewise until he became distracted by the waves. It is a true statement that, if you don't lose focus on Jesus, you will never sink in the ocean of life. Again, as long as your faith is intact, you will remain afloat.

"And straightway Jesus constrained his disciples to get into a ship, and to go before him unto the other side, while He sent the multitudes away. And when He had sent the multitudes away, He went up into a mountain apart to pray: and when the evening was come, He was there alone. But the ship was now in the midst of the sea, tossed with waves: for the wind was contrary. And in the fourth watch of the night Jesus went unto them, walking on the sea. And when the disciples saw Him walking on the sea, they were troubled, saying, 'It is a spirit;' and they cried out for fear. But straightway Jesus spake unto them, saying, 'Be of good cheer; it is I; be not afraid.' And Peter answered him and said, 'Lord, if it be thou, bid me come unto thee on the water.' And He said, 'Come.' And when Peter was come down out of

the ship, he walked on the water, to go to Jesus. But when he saw the wind boisterous, he was afraid; and beginning to sink, he cried, saying, 'Lord, save me.' And immediately Jesus stretched forth His hand, and caught him, and said unto him, 'O thou of little faith, wherefore didst thou doubt?' And when they were come into the ship, the wind ceased. Then they that were in the ship came and worshipped him, saying, 'Of a truth thou art the Son of God' (**Matt. 14:22-33**).

Peter had seen the Lord Jesus walk on water and he wanted to do the same. Personally, Peter knew it was humanly impossible, but he was a man of faith. He wanted to follow His Master, and his desire propelled him to humbly solicit for an invitation from the Lord.

Fortunately, Jesus gave him the command to come. When he was asked to come, he was willing to trust the Lord and walk on the surface of the water with Him. Although, he knew he could drown, his faith and focus sustained him. As long as he fixed his eyes on the Lord Jesus, Peter was able to walk on the water, but once he got distracted by the waves, he began to sink.

The Lord in His infinite mercy rescued him by pulling him into the boat. Many of us today have the same issue that Peter had. The distractions around us are diverting our gaze, thus making us sink.

However, even though we get distracted, there is hope as long as we quickly redirect our focus on Jesus. You can always look back to Him and remind yourself of His promises, love and faithfulness. The Lord Jesus is always there for us, standing with open arms to receive us.

At this point, I believe we will derive a lot of encouragement from the following hymn composed by Helen Howarth Lemmel in 1922:

1. O soul, are you weary and troubled?
No light in the darkness you see?
There's light for a look at the Savior,
And life more abundant and free!
Refrain:
Turn your eyes upon Jesus,
Look full in His wonderful face,
And the things of earth will grow strangely dim,
In the light of His glory and grace.
2. Through death into life everlasting
He passed, and we follow Him there;
O'er us sin no more hath dominion—
For more than conqu'rors we are!
3. His Word shall not fail you—He promised;
Believe Him, and all will be well:
Then go to a world that is dying,
His perfect salvation to tell!

CHAPTER 10

SEEKING DIVINE GUIDANCE

The devil has designed well-constructed traps operated via his various distractive strategies in a manner that seemingly leaves little or no room for escape. He has intertwined his evil ways in the routine activities of life that even if we try to recover from his noose, we somehow end up falling into his satanic setup. The worst part is that even in this unending battle, the preferred route of escape for people of our generation is taking solace in their own wisdom or temporal refuge in other distractions that comfort them in times of struggle.

Ignorantly, most of us tend to isolate ourselves totally from the world, and we think that we will remain unharmed from the gallows of the enemy. What we fail to realize is that in our isolation, we also tend to abandon God and this temporal detachment will slowly escort us back to the doorpost of the devil. Despite knowing the power of God's Word and the dire need of staying focused on Him, we always turn a blind eye to His guidance. Thus, the devil continues to rule over our lives in different forms and keeps us away from staying in fellowship with God.

There are various reasons for the widespread rebellion against God's guidance, but all of it comes down to man's inclination towards sin and withdrawal from the love of God. Since the beginning of time, God's guidance is freely made available to whoever seeks Him.

Let God guide you

"'Then shall ye call upon Me, and ye shall go and pray unto Me, and I will hearken unto you. And ye shall seek Me, and find Me, when ye shall search for Me with all your heart. And I will be found of you,' saith the Lord, 'and I will turn away your captivity, and I will gather you from all the nations, and from all the places whither I have driven you,' saith the Lord, 'and I will bring you again into the place whence I caused you to be carried away captive'" (**Jer. 29:12-14**).

The Lord has promised liberation from captivity and sanctification from the pollution of the world. These promises and their fulfillments are seen in the biblical account of how God faithfully guided His people towards their destinations.

The story of how God guided Abraham to where He established His covenant with him or that of Moses and the Israelites, who were led out of the land of servitude, made it clear that God has never disappointed His people, but always fulfills His promises.

Although, pushing these famous accounts of deliverance and fulfillment of promises aside, you will still find other inspiring stories of people like Noah, Lot, Jonah, and Ruth who were perfectly guided by the Lord. These people diligently sought Him in an age where the rest of the world's population were drifting away from truth and giving in to sin, similar to the state of the world today. However, the only reason these few men and women of God stood out from among the mammoth crowd was their willingness to listen to, follow and obey God.

Therefore, it is right to conclude that, if people have sunk into their sinfulness, it is only because they have tried to find guidance in other places, rather than God. Examples of people who surrendered to the captivity of the devil and equally tried to find guidance from evil sources are not uncommon in the Bible.

DANGERS OF UNGUIDED LIFE

"So Saul died for his transgression which he committed against the Lord, even against the word of the Lord, which he kept not, and also for asking counsel of one that had a familiar spirit, to inquire of it" **(1 Chro. 10:13).**

Saul had not only consulted a demonic medium to gain guidance, but he presumptuously refused to keep God's Word. The Lord had severally given him commands that he disregarded and as a result of His disobedience, he met an untimely death.

Even today, despite the rapidity of the spread of the gospel, mighty manifestations in many churches and innumerable promises of God for this end time, many people are still trying to seek guidance from sinful and ungodly sources. Ignorantly, while some seek it in the opinions and suggestions of the world, there are some who are actively involved in witchcraft and other satanic rituals.

The number of people involved in these activities is soaring and it cannot be denied that this still exists and with time, satanic worship will also increase. There are cults and evil practices that people try their best to hide. But today, satanists have come into the open. They boldly confess their allegiance to Satan. Some are in academia, politics, film industry, to mention just a few. In fact, the Church of Satan has been established in a couple of states in the United States. These people follow Satan because of what he offers to them as a reward for their worship.

In all fairness, if it is true that the majority of the world is far from these practices, why is it that the world continues to go deeper into sin? This is because even though the devil's plans are evidently projected around the world, he craftily camouflages himself under the seemingly harmless activities.

As we have previously learned about technology, media and the attractiveness of materialism, we can see that the enemy uses all sorts of ways to keep us occupied in trivial matters. He does not necessarily have to use evil ways, but the smallest activity that prioritizes itself above God is one that is sent from him.

Consequently, we would end up being drawn away from the true God, who alone can shepherd us through the straight and narrow way. God is the only one that can give us clear vision in this misty world of sin. If we think we can do anything without His assistance, then we are grossly mistaken. Therefore, if we intend to keep away from the sinfulness of the world and really want to live eternally with our Creator, then we must submit to the guidance of the Holy Spirit.

"For as many as are led by the Spirit of God, they are the sons of God" (**Rom.8:14**).

There are many people today trying to find refuge in different kinds of places, aside from the Word of God. They look for discernment and knowledge about what they must do, but they consider the Word of God as the last option and sometimes, totally neglect it. This is mostly because they ridicule the idea of the relevance of God's Word in the current humanistic era. God intends that the Holy Bible should be our guide in every situation of life.

THE HOLY BIBLE: THE ASTONISHING WORD

The Bible is so rich in wisdom and astounding stories that boggle our minds. This great book contains an account of multitudinous people traveling to another nation. They suddenly encountered a red sea, while a powerful army was chasing them. Miraculously, the raging sea was parted, and all their stubborn pursuers were baptized to death.

Again, there is a story of a man called Daniel who survived in the den of lions. Also, Shadrach, Meshach, and Abednego emerged unhurt from Nebuchadnezzar's fiery furnace. Besides, there was also an incident of a man named Jonah, who was swallowed by a giant fish, which later vomited him where God wanted him to be.

Apart from all these, there are many other stories of miracles and wonders that are very rare in this modern world, but they are packed in the pages of this miracle book called the Holy Bible. This is why many people think that the book has lost its effect, and that biblical guidance is outdated. According to them, the Word is no longer applicable to our lives as we now live in a digitalized, fast-paced world where guidance is sought online via search engines. Alas, this is how the enemy cleverly removed the importance of God's

Word by putting false beliefs in people's minds regarding the credibility and potency of the Word of God.

Regrettably, the enemy has negatively convinced most people to the extent that they are far separated from the wonderful experiences of the previous generations. Our failure was caused by social and scientific advancement; hence, we have become cheap victims of life's challenges. Therefore, finding direction for how to lead our daily lives in a book that was written centuries ago is considered a foolish idea.

However, the truth remains that the Word of God is a complete guide and approved roadmap for the people who have lost their ways. It contains answers to the most profound philosophical questions such as how the world was created, what happens after death, and how we must relate with God and our neighbors. It is a beacon of light that spreads out to all who have strayed away from the Lord and sincerely want to come back to the right path of righteousness.

The Bible may be underestimated, but it is the only source of true wisdom and guidance. No matter how much the devil tries to mislead the people of God, the Word is always there to lead them back to the right path. If we allow God to take over our decisions, then we will see how the evil one will lose his grip on us, and we will stay close to the Lord.

A great example of divine guidance takes us back to the Christmas story that includes the three wise men that were guided by a star to where Jesus was born. The three wise men were Magi, which was an order of the Pagan MedoPersian religious order of Zoroaster. The Magi were ancient interpreters of dreams and were astrologers (monthly prognosticators), enchanters, sorcerers, and magicians.

These men did not know where the child (Christ) was, but they had to stay focused on the lone star until it eventually led them to the manger where the Baby was laid. These three wise men saw the natal star of Jesus, which shifted their whole focus from other stars to that lone star. They focused on it and followed it to where the promised King was kept. The wise men likely traveled with a large number of attendants and guards for their long journey, which would have taken several weeks.

According to history, if they had come from Babylon through the main trade route of about 800 miles (1,288 kilometers), averaging 20 miles (32 kilometers) per day, the trip would have taken about 40 days. They continued their long journey because their eyes were fixated on the star.

Furthermore, these three wise men were scholars; therefore, they had access to the writings of Daniel, who was a high official of the royal government of Babylon. They were highly significant, because only high government officials or high religious leaders had access to books, since there was no printing press at that time. To crown it all, they knew about this King who was about to be born. Their focus was so intense that they did not have to look for any other medium, but God Himself through the Star that guided them to Jesus.

Similarly, the story of the Israelites whom the Lord guided through a pillar of fire during the night and thick cloud during the day is another remarkable guidance of the Almighty. The Lord has various ways of leading His people, but all we need to do is to trust Him wholly without any other idol in our hearts.

"Trust in the Lord with all thine heart; and lean not unto thine own understanding. In all thy ways acknowledge him, and he shall direct thy paths" (**Prov. 3:5-6**).

He is always ready and willing to help us, but we must completely accept His guidance and come out of the distraction that the devil has placed in our lives.

Unknown to people, the enemy has perfected his strategies in such a way to prevent people from coming to the Lord, even if it is the last resort. His objective is to preclude us from living a victorious life in Christ. Therefore, it is imperative that no matter how far we have strayed away, we should always return to the Lord and ask Him to guide us when life puzzles us. Our God is a God of a second chance.

Perhaps, you are going through some frustrations in your life; maybe you've lost sight of the guiding star or the pillar of cloud and pillar of fire, and you need to regain your vision by looking into His Word, which is our surest source of light in a dark world. Just like the guiding Star in the silent night of the birth of Jesus and the pillar of fire for the Israelites in the wilderness of temptations, the Word of God is always there to show you the path ahead.

THE SUPREMACY OF GOD'S KNOWLEDGE

God knows the way that lies before you. He knows the pitfall and where the enemy has mounted some roadblocks against you. No matter how wise we may consider ourselves to be, we have to admit that He is an all-knowing and all-powerful God, who is not only aware of the plans of the enemy, but also has the power to overthrow his kingdom and thwart his plans.

"And he said, 'Nay, but as captain of the host of the Lord am I now come.' And Joshua fell on his face to the earth, and did worship, and said unto him, 'What saith my lord unto his servant?' (**Josh. 5:14**).

Today, we have the omnipotent Spirit of the Lord that can stand up for our cause. He is always there to assist us, so that we no longer remain losers, but winners: peculiar people, living courageously with a specific direction in life.

As this Heavenly Commander removed all obstacles standing between Israel and their Promised Land, the Red Sea, river Jordan and the tall walls of Jericho, He is here to clear the way before you. All you need to do is to be an obedient child of God and humbly submit to His leadership, as Joshua did. Beloved, you should willfully ask for His guidance, and He will stretch out His hand to lead you.

The secret of Prophet Jeremiah's success in life and ministry was his full understanding of the futility of trusting in one's own beliefs and opinions. He understood the need for God's direction and guidance in everything he did; therefore, he escaped many dangers and subsequently became a revelation channel.

"O Lord, I know that the way of man is not in himself: it is not in man that walketh to direct his steps" (**Jer. 10:23**).

All our attempts to tackle the darts of the devil and live successfully on earth are foolish ideas stemming from deep-seated pride in us. We can only win if we trust the Lord and walk according to His will. There are numerous ways that God talks to us today. We only need to be attentive to Him and recognize His voice like the sheep recognizes the voice of their shepherd.

In addition to finding Him in our daily lives, we must always go back to His Word to know what He wants from us. His Word contains answers to our deepest questions that no one else can answer. Therefore, trust in Him and His guidance, because His promises are absolutely dependable.

"I will go before thee, and make the crooked places straight; I will break in pieces the gates of brass, and cut in sunder the bars of iron; and I will give thee the treasures of darkness, and hidden riches of secret places, that thou mayest know that I, the Lord, which call thee by thy name, am the God of Israel" **(Is. 45:2-3).**

<u>THERE IS HOPE FOR YOU</u>

We have a loving God who stands with outstretched arms to accept us back. He calls each one of us by our name and He is willing to transform our lives. If you think that you have extremely strayed away from Him, you are absolutely wrong. That thought itself originated from Satan and it was designed to keep you away from His grace forever.

But you must know that His mercy is abundant to anyone who comes, and it is never too late to surrender to the Lord and ask Him to lead you like He has been leading His people throughout the ages.

"All that the Father giveth me shall come to me; and him that cometh to me I will in no wise cast out" **(Jn. 6:37).**

In this sinful and grief-stricken world, our only hope is in the Lord's deliverance. Therefore, I urge you to allow Him to take over your life and lead you through the rocky road with the guidance of His Word.

CHAPTER 11

TAKE HEART, HE HAS OVERCOME

As the epidemic of sin permeates the entire surface of the earth and the ruler of the world successfully prevails with his demonic strategies, there seems to be little hope that the state of the world will ever be renewed. The dominion of the evil one grows stronger with each passing day, and the world continues to march down the path of destruction.

Therefore, amidst this sinfulness and innumerable distractions, it remains a struggle to battle against Satan's assaults as he constantly tries to shift our focus from Jesus towards the fleeting pleasures of sin. He tries to keep us so pre-occupied with the thrills of the world that we slowly drift away from God's presence and allow sin to rule over every area of our life. And so, being surrounded by the tactics of the devil veneered in a false sense of fulfillment and joy, it becomes harder to keep ourselves untainted by sin.

<u>OUR ULTIMATE HOPE</u>

As we draw close to the end of our journey of learning about Satan's strategies to colonize the earth, it is crucial that we also recognize the hope we have in Jesus Christ. Indeed, the state of the world tends to fill our hearts with fear as we see how the condition only deteriorates with time. However, the Lord has promised us His peace and restoration amidst the uncertainty, and this is what we will learn in this final chapter.

Keeping this seemingly endless battle with the evil one in mind, you may be troubled by the conundrum whether the fight against these strategies will persist forever, or will the creature ever see redemption again. Will the world ever be restored back to the initial state, or will it go down its path of impending doom? First, we need to realize the fact that God's original plan was not to make the world become a sorrow-inducing place. God had created a world which was flooded with His glory and man could freely experience the joy of His presence. However, when sin entered, it separated man from enjoying unbridled fellowship with God.

We may have heard and even studied about this eternal separation, but it is essential to understand the underlying universal defeat behind this entire picture. When man disobeyed God, it was not just a loss of freedom or advent of death. It was an eternal detachment from the holy presence of God. It was a self-inflicted punishment that came as a result of their disobedience towards God. It was Satan himself that tempted man to commit this great sin and it was never the will of God to banish mankind from His presence. But since man rebelled against God and defied His orders, man's defiance became something that was abominable in God's eyes; thus, man suffered its due consequences.

Now, despite the depravity of man and the abounding wretchedness, God could not bear the thought of losing them eternally. He wanted to bring them back to Himself and restore the broken bond between Him and mankind. Thus, after the dawn of a dark and corrupt world, He promised to send a King that will overcome all the evil plans of the devil. He will overthrow the wicked kingdom and renew the state of creation by bringing an end to death and giving hope of access to everlasting life with God once again.

Immediately man sinned, God pronounced the punishment and as well foretold the coming of a Messiah, who will release mankind from this punishment. The Savior will bail human beings from their sentence to prison on earth and will also bring a final end to satanic colonization.

"And I will put enmity between thee and the woman, and between thy seed and her seed; it shall bruise thy head, and thou shalt bruise his heel" (**Gen. 3:15**).

Here, God pronounced judgment upon the serpent, the most "cunning of all the beasts of the field," while also foretelling the culmination. This was the restoration prophesy that gave hope to the coming generation, who sought riddance from the power of sin.

THE PROPHETS AND THE MESSIAH

The Book of Isaiah also mentions the coming of the messianic King that will salvage mankind from all effects of sin. Isaiah Chapter 53 artistically paints the portrait of this King, who takes up the punishment of the world and suffers its brutality as a substitute for the rest of humanity.

"Surely he hath borne our griefs, and carried our sorrows: yet we did esteem him stricken, smitten of God, and afflicted. But he was wounded for our transgressions; he was bruised for our iniquities; the chastisement of our peace was upon him; and

with his stripes we are healed. All we like sheep have gone astray; we have turned every one to his own way; and the Lord hath laid on him the iniquity of us all **(Is. 53:4-6)**.

In fact, this is what the fulfillment of the prophecy looks like, but none of the kings from the lineage of David went through this. In fact, sacrificing themselves was a far-fetched idea for them, as they were so driven by the sinful pleasures of this world. The distractions of Satan successfully enticed them to rebel against the commands of God.

Based on this, even if they repented, they could never denounce sin completely. They felt weak to its effects and the hereditary nature transferred from one to another like an incurable disease. Death continued to dig its claws as sin was enthroned by man against the will of God.

It was apparent that none of the kings could master the strategies of the devil, and a kingdom that was supposed to restore the original state of mankind was used for the establishment of the satanic government. With no one to fulfill the promise, it seemed like the plan was lost. It looked like the prophecy will never find fulfillment; hence, it was a dismal defeat for man, when they failed to find restoration among human leaders.

During this Dark Age, there were men and women of God who hoped for the coming of this Messiah. These prophets continued to prophesy about this King, who would overthrow the reign of satanic captivity and fulfill the promise mentioned in the Book of Genesis. These people had hope that God was going to relieve them of all the wrongs happening in their world.

Equally, they were persuaded that the ancient serpent would be trampled on and totally defeated, so that he could no longer exhibit power over humanity. Satan was going to lose his authority and fall on his knees as the King of kings would overcome him for His people.

THE AWESOME PRICE OF REDEMPTION

Now, this ultimate victory would not just come on a platter of gold. There was an underlying puzzle and an extremely hard nut to crack. An unfathomable price would be paid. Who would pay the price?

A condition was placed on this promised victory. When the victory over the devil would occur, the messianic King would suffer the punishment that man deserved. The Bible reveals how the Seed of the woman tramples over the head of the serpent, and the serpent bites the heel of the Seed of the woman. This depicts how the promised King would take the punishment of all evils perpetrated by humanity and suffer the fatal consequence of death. However, the Bible reiterates that this horrible death marks the beginning of a hope-filled future. After the attack, the King would rise again and overcome the sting of death. He would come back to life and then become a source of healing to others. Thus, the Old Testament ended with this prophecy, and the people were left waiting for this Messiah, who would take away their shame and reproach. He is going to set them apart as righteous people, because of His own sacrifice and blot out their transgressions once and for all.

PROPHECY FULFILLED

It seems the story had ended when the New Testament began and showed us a picture of a Man from the lineage of Abraham, Judah and David. Although, He was not born in a royal family (ruling house), He still emanated from the bloodline of kings, which was a fulfillment of God's Word. He was the snakecrushing King that the Old Testament's patriarchs and matriarchs waited for, but He never came.

Amazingly, when it seemed there was no hope and Satan's evil plans were reaching new heights, it happened. The prophecy finally came true. The Savior, who was meant to save us, fulfilled the ancient promises made in the Torah and the prophetic word of God. From the beginning, the people had been waiting for Him to come and restore them, and now, He has finally come.

He came, dwelt among men, and preached to them about the hope and restoration of God's Kingdom. He told them that God's Kingdom is already here, and He started confronting the effects of evil that people were suffering from. Some of the distractions that we see in the present age also existed then too, such as fear, anxiety, the enticement of lust, pleasures and possessions.

Jesus openly spoke about these very issues. He preached in the streets and warned people of the effects of sin, showing them a better way of repentance and fellowship with God, by forsaking earthly pleasures. He healed the sick and also forgave them their sins, showing that He had the power to remove the effects of the evil spread by the serpent.

Jesus, the promised King, was among men and He was to take the sins of humanity upon Himself by suffering on the cross, and He did. Due to His love and power, He took the fatal snake bite and it seemed Satan had won. It was like the power of the devil had defeated the Messiah. This story would have indeed been a tragic one if it ended in the grave.

Praise God! The case was reversed. The serpent did not win, even after attacking the Messiah. Instead, Jesus rose again on the third day. He gloriously rose and proved that he had power over death, as well as the evil plots of the enemy. He overcame it all for our sake.

Now, this question may be boiling in your heart that, if He has overcome the world, why is the devil still successful in his plans? Why does he still continue to reign over the people and lure them into sin with his evil strategies? Why are people still surrounded by these various distractions that keep them away from God? This is because the devil has power over the present world. He is currently the ruler of this dark world. He has authority over it, but his dominion is short-lived.

How to partake in His victory

Now, the question arises about how the death and suffering of the Messiah could lead to the salvation of humanity. Apostle Paul made it known in his letter to the Romans that all have sinned and come short of the glory of God. All truly means all, including the poor and the rich, noble and common, regardless of race, color, age, nationality and status (see Romans 3:23).

"For the wages of sin is death" **(Rom. 6:23).**

Therefore, all human beings are condemned to death because of their sins. However, by shedding His blood on the cross, Jesus took the punishment we deserved and offered us His righteousness. When we trust Christ for our salvation, we are offered a divine exchange. By faith, we exchange our sin and its accompanying death penalty for His righteousness and everlasting life.

"For he hath made him to be sin for us, who knew no sin; that we might be made the righteousness of God in him" (**2 Cor. 5:21**).

In theology, this process is referred to as "substitutionary atonement." Christ died on the cross as our substitute. Without Him, we would suffer the death penalty for our own sins.

"For God so loved the world, that he gave his only begotten Son, that whosoever believeth in him should not perish, but have everlasting life" (**Jn. 3:16**).

Hallelujah! The power that Jesus gained over sin and death is made available to us as well. We can also get access to eternal life and authority gained over Satan as long as we are on earth. While distractions continue to influence people around us, the victory through Christ is made available to us in this turbulent world.

However, we can only make use of this available grace and live a triumphant life by surrendering our lives to Jesus, the Savior.

"Therefore being justified by faith, we have peace with God through our Lord Jesus Christ: by whom also we have access by faith into this grace wherein we stand, and rejoice in hope of the glory of God" (**Rom. 5:1-2**).

Therefore, through the grace of God, victory is ours! Yet, it is sad that death and evil continue to prevail in our present broken world, with the serpent constantly trying to make us forget the power that we have in Jesus. He occupies us with diverse distractions that we have studied about.

Due to distractions, we are hindered from fixing our eyes on Jesus. This may be disheartening, yet the Bible tells us to cheer up and rejoice in His glorious coming.

<u>VICTORY REASSURED</u>

The story has not ended, and the best state of the creation is yet to be restored. The Bible talks about a future day when Jesus will come back and bring the entire work to completion. He will destroy the serpent once and for all, and equally restore the relationship of man with God once again.

"These things I have spoken unto you, that in me ye might have peace. In the world ye shall have tribulation, but be of good cheer; I have overcome the world" **(Jn. 16:33).**

We have His peace planted in our hearts. So, we need not fret about certain doom ahead of mankind. We have hope in Jesus that even though Satan tries to distract us, our focus won't shift from our Lord and Savior, Jesus Christ. Sometimes, when persecution comes our way, we must not allow this to distract us, because it is for a fleeting moment. We must remember that Jesus suffered greater persecutions and He has transferred His total victory to us. We can always look to Him for reassurance that we are victorious, and that the present situation is only an interlude and is not the end of the story.

Above all, He reminds us of our eternal placement in heaven and how we are not of this world.

"If the world hates you, ye know that it hated me before it hated you. If ye were of the world, the world would love his own; but because ye are not of the world, but I have chosen you out of the world, therefore the world hateth you" **(Jn. 15:18-19).**

Thus, we can feel reassured by His peace. He has conquered it all, and even removed the wall of partition that once separated us from God. He removed the enmity, and now He grants us power with faith to overcome all the fiery darts of the evil one. He has completed the work of reconciliation and we are now His own and citizens of the Kingdom of God as stated in the book of Ephesians.

"Wherefore remember, that ye being in time past Gentiles in the flesh, who are called Uncircumcision by that which is called the Circumcision in the flesh made by hands; That at that time ye were without Christ, being aliens from the commonwealth of Israel, and strangers from the covenants of promise, having no hope, and without God in the world: But now in Christ Jesus ye who sometimes were far off are made nigh by the blood of Christ. For he is our peace, who hath made both one, and hath broken down the middle wall of partition between us; Having abolished in his flesh the enmity, even the law of commandments contained in ordinances; for to make in himself of twain one new man, so making peace; And that he might reconcile both unto God in one body by the cross, having slain the enmity thereby:And came and preached peace to you which were afar off, and to them that were nigh. For through him we both have access by one Spirit unto the Father. Now therefore ye are no more strangers and foreigners, but fellow citizens with the saints, and of the household of God; And are built upon the foundation of the apostles and prophets, Jesus Christ himself being the chief corner stone; In whom all the building fitly framed together groweth unto an holy temple in the Lord" **(Ephesians 2:11-21).**

CONCLUSION

So far, you have seen and read a series of comforting thoughts from this book and also from the Holy Bible, the indisputable and inexhaustible word of God. This remains the strongest anchor in a world that is flooded with sin and godlessness. Surely, we can still walk with the Lord by recognizing the power of His Word, praying diligently and using the word of God as the sword of the Spirit to combat any foe. Amidst all of the aforementioned distractions, it is paramount that we keep our eyes perfectly fixed on Jesus, the Author and Finisher of our faith.

Despite all odds, we should encourage ourselves through the cloud of witnesses that have gone before us and are also cheering us to run the race successfully to the finish line, by defying all odds. Realistically, as you shield yourself with His grace, you will soon discover that He will purify you and set you apart from the corruptions of this broken world.

Keep pressing; never relent from pushing, because as you begin to spend quality time with God in fellowship and you are striving to walk closely with Him on daily basis, the devil will certainly try to pull you back to the world, and to his kingdom of darkness.

However, looking to the Word of God as a lighthouse in the middle of the sea will take you to your anticipated destination. All that is needed is to remain obedient till your last breath. You need to continue to walk in holiness and surrender your life to Him. But you cannot do this without the support of a Bible believing Church. Seek one near you and fully commit to her membership. The closer you are to God, the more the distractions of the satanic world will lose their grip on you. Therefore, you need to remain steadfast in your faith in the Lord Jesus, and cling to the great hope that very soon, He will appear to restore mankind to his glorious state, which is in tandem with His original plan for man. Till then, we have His peace to comfort our hearts and give us the courage to carry on.

"Peace I leave with you; my peace I give unto you. Not as the world giveth, give I unto you. Let not your heart be troubled, neither let it be afraid. Ye have heard how I said unto you, I go away, and come again unto you. If ye loved me, ye would rejoice, because I said, I go unto the Father: for my Father is greater than I" **(Jn. 14:27-28).**

Always remember that the solid foundation of spiritual life that will guarantee physical success and eternal life is strong faith in the Lord Jesus Christ.

www.ingramcontent.com/pod-product-compliance
Lightning Source LLC
Chambersburg PA
CBHW051205120626
46547CB00013B/1214